WHEN THE WINDS BLOW

Also by Derek Tangye

TIME WAS MINE
ONE KING
WENT THE DAY WELL (editor)

The Minack Chronicles

A GULL ON THE ROOF
A CAT IN THE WINDOW
A DRAKE AT THE DOOR
A DONKEY IN THE MEADOW
LAMA
THE WAY TO MINACK
A CORNISH SUMMER
COTTAGE ON A CLIFF
A CAT AFFAIR
SUN ON THE LINTEL
SOMEWHERE A CAT IS WAITING (*Omnibus*)
THE WINDING LANE

Derek Tangye

WHEN THE WINDS BLOW

ILLUSTRATED BY JEAN TANGYE

London
MICHAEL JOSEPH

First published in Great Britain by Michael Joseph Ltd
44 Bedford Square, London WC1B 3DU
1980

ISBN 0 7181 1932 0

Set and printed in Great Britain by
Ebenezer Baylis and Son Ltd
The Trinity Press, Worcester, and London
and bound by Redwood Burn, Esher

To Eric Hiscock
from us both

ONE

I went out of the door, and dusk was falling, and the wind was beginning to stir from the west. I went past the *escallonia*, night dormitory of the dunnocks, to the terrace we call the bridge, then up two steps into the Lama field, where we grow the Joseph Macleod daffodils, and then turned left until I reached the stone and earth hedge, on top of which I have repeatedly tried to grow a bed of flowers. From here, on clear days, the whole sweep of Mount's Bay can be seen and marvelled at . . . and my failure to grow a bed of flowers is unnoticed.

Only Jeannie's catmint has blossomed. The plant came from her green-fingered Aunt Lorna, who used to have a nursery in Bristol and whose plants are in various corners of our garden. The catmint, in due course, became the cats' pub. Ambrose sneaked to it, Oliver adored it . . . and that evening of November, when the wind was beginning to stir and I was standing close beside it, the Lizard Light already blinking, the sky above Culdrose Air Station becoming a rose red, factory fishing boats blazing with lights in between, I suddenly became aware of Oliver beside me. Oliver loved me ('Make a friend of a cat,' someone has said, 'and you *have* a friend'), and he had a knack of following me when I least expected it, when I hadn't seen him around, then suddenly appearing,

7

as he did on this occasion, at my feet. I had a mission to perform. He had come to share it.

As I stood there, he brushed his head against my leg; but when I, wishing to show my appreciation, bent down to stroke him, he jumped away perversely, up on the hedge, and straight to the catmint. He began nibbling the leaves. That instant, if Jeannie had been with me, she would have said: 'Don't drink too much!' Then, satisfied, he turned on his back, rolling his black person upon it . . . just at the moment I was fulfilling the purpose of my coming out of the cottage that November evening. The purpose to watch, unobserved, Fred and Mingoose Merlin in the field overlooking the sea below the hedge, on their first evening together.

Fred had been waiting ten months for a companion. Penny, his mother, had died one early January morning. Penny, the gentle black donkey who had come to Minack fifteen years before, and who had given birth to Fred within a month of her arrival. Fred had been waiting, hooting frequently during the day, and sometimes at night. Fred, who always dutifully followed his mother as she roamed the meadows, was bewildered at being alone.

It was my fault, Jeannie's too for that matter, that had prevented him having a new companion. Both of us share an attitude towards the ending of a long companionship, which may be old-fashioned, illogical and over-sentimental. It is that we cannot replace a long companionship with the same ease as replacing a smashed teapot. We need, for a while, to remain loyal to the memory, to prove that love was sincere, not an indulgence.

The summer, therefore, was coming to an end before my mind began to wander around the idea of looking for a companion for Fred. I did not, however, take any practical steps. I had a lazy notion that the matter would be solved without effort, that someone perhaps would arrive at the door pleading for a home for a donkey. This would have suited us. The situation would have forced us to make a decision. But no one came to the door.

There was also the question as to how Fred would react to the presence of a donkey companion. Supposing he hated the sight of it? Supposing the donkey hated the sight of Fred? He may have been lonely but, as with human beings, the wrong companion could prove to be far more distressing than loneliness. Fred was now king of the meadows: wandered about at will, received special privileges, such as walking up the winding lane without a halter when we went to fetch the milk from the farm; and when visitors called, there was no competition for their admiration. He alone received their praise, their carrots, their chocolate biscuits; no rival in sight.

But, when autumn came and dusk fell earlier and earlier, and the period when Fred was alone in the dark became longer, it was obvious that we could not wait for a donkey to arrive at the door. We had to go out and search for one. A task, now we had made up our minds, we expected to be a quick and easy one. Yet, as often happens when at last one has decided upon some certain action, the opportunity to take such action fails to materialise.

We scanned 'animals for sale' advertisements in local newspapers, and a donkey was never mentioned. We had word that a donkey was for sale at Zennor, on the north coast of West Cornwall, then found he was a prize stallion; but Fred was a gelding, and it was a gelding that we were looking for. Another message sent us to Leedstown, between Penzance and Helston, where the donkey awaiting our inspection was a mare in foal. We went one day to find Roy Teague, the one-time publican who had sold us Penny, and who was still a dealer in horses and donkeys. He was at Helston market, we were told at his home, and we drove to Helston and wandered around the market, asking for him, but he was nowhere to be found. Had we found him (he later wrote offering us *three* donkeys), Mingoose Merlin would never have come into our lives because, an hour later, back at Minack, I opened the Donkey Breed Society's *News Letter* and saw the advertisement we were looking for:

'MINGOOSE MERLIN, large brown 18-months-old registered gelding, by ROMANY OF HUNTERS BROOK, ex-prize winning mare. Very successfully shown, excellent potential for driving. Kind, knowledgeable home for this exceptionally handsome and lovable donkey my first consideration. Mrs V. Bailey, The Forge, Skinners Bottom, Redruth, Cornwall.'

The address had a special appeal for Jeannie. Skinners Bottom was only a couple of miles away from the field where, those years ago, we had collected Penny. We had backed the Land Rover against a make-shift earth ramp and Penny had walked up it into the well of the Land Rover, and had come back with us to Minack, head resting on my shoulder as I drove; serene, seemingly confident she was going to a home that her destiny meant her to go to. Always when we pass that field, now cut away by the Redruth by-pass, except for a small section of it, one of us will say: 'We're passing Penny land.'

Thus, when Mingoose Merlin's address was given as Skinners Bottom, he belonged, so to speak, already to Minack. We had become impatient to acquire a companion for Fred. We had had false starts in looking for one, but now, for the simple reason that Mingoose Merlin was quartered in the vicinity of the place where our donkey experiences began, we were certain, after reading the advertisement, that we would acquire him.

I did, however, have some doubts. I had never, for instance, intended to have an aristocratic donkey as a companion for Fred. I had hoped for one of those donkeys which had been badly treated, which had no recorded ancestry, to which one of the admirable donkey sanctuaries would have given a home had they been aware of the situation. Such a donkey, I felt, would have been suitable for Fred. They would have shared an anonymity. Together they would have been a couple of donkeys who came from a long line of unknown donkeys which had trod the bogs of Ireland. A touch of sadness would have united them.

Mingoose Merlin's background, however, was impeccable. Jingle Bells, his mother, was a Show donkey; and his father, Romany of Hunters Brook, had appeared in the advertisement pages of the Donkey Breed Society as one of the most sought after stallions of his time. Mingoose Merlin, in fact, was a very favoured donkey. It was as if he had rich parents who had sent him to fashionable schools. He wasn't a hobbledehoy like Fred. Mingoose Merlin was *registered*. There, in the Donkey Breed Society's *Stud Book*, was written his aristocratic lineage. Fred had no chance at all of being included in such a Stud Book.

I was, too, at the time, although a member, a little suspicious of the purpose of the Donkey Breed Society. I wondered whether it was not an outlet for socially ambitious people. People who took more pleasure in entering their donkeys at Shows than in loving them. I have never been in tune with those people, whether dog-owners, cat-owners, bird fanciers, or any other animal owner, who become besotted by the desire to *show* their pet. The vanity of the owner seems to take over. The pet becomes the vehicle of human ambition.

However, I am now wiser about the Donkey Breed Society, and every donkey owner should be a member, and even those who would like to be donkey owners, but can never be because of the circumstances in which they live. The Society enlightens you on every aspect of the donkey world, acts as a guardian against donkey cruelty, and its annual magazine is a donkey owner's bible . . . and, in any case, as far as Jeannie and I are concerned, it is due to the Society that Mingoose Merlin (Merlin to his friends) came to Minack.

He had arrived that morning . . . on a week's trial. He had been driven in a horsebox from Skinners Bottom and been deposited outside the farm buildings at the top of our lane, where Jeannie and I were waiting. Accompanying him had come the two people who hitherto had been most concerned with his life, Jenifer Hilliard, who had bred him, and Val Bailey, who was selling him, and their presence made me feel uncomfortable. They both clearly adored Merlin. Val, Jenifer's neighbour, was only selling him because she had an old donkey, and Merlin was too boisterous to be a suitable companion. Their presence made me feel I was a usurper; that although I had paid my cheque, we did not own Merlin. Merlin, I felt at this moment of his arrival, was like a house I might have rented; the rent paid by me, but the ownership was elsewhere. Once again I wished it was an anonymous donkey that was to be Fred's companion. A donkey whose previous owner we did not know, instead of a donkey whose first eighteen months had been spent a bare twenty miles away.

Merlin did not care. He had emerged without fuss from the horsebox, consumed the presentation carrots we had ready for him, then, as if he knew exactly where he was going, set off down the winding lane, Jeannie holding the halter, and Jenifer Hilliard, Val Bailey and myself in pursuit.

He had an unusual appearance. I had scarcely observed him when we had gone to Skinners Bottom to inspect him. I was so anxious not to dither, so anxious to acquire him before I had time to change my mind, that I only noticed how woolly he was before Jeannie and I were in the car and away. Now, as he hurried down the lane with Jeannie, his woolly brown coat looked so long that he reminded me of a yak, and it so covered his legs that he looked as if he were wearing old-fashioned plus-fours. He went faster and faster down the lane, Jeannie scarcely able to hold him, then round the final bend and along to Monty's Leap, the little stream which crosses our lane, which he jumped as if he were in a race, up past the barn where, without hesitation, he turned left. And there, at the gate, was Fred.

They peered at each other over the bar, like two boxers weighing each other up.

'Fred,' I said, 'this is Merlin.'

I was also aware of another dimension in the situation. It was as if Jeannie and I were in one corner as seconds for Fred, Jenifer and Val in the other corner as seconds for Merlin. No aggro, of course, just a wish on our part that Fred should not yield to the character of Merlin, and on theirs that Merlin should not yield to the character of Fred.

'Let's open the gate,' I said.

It was a beautiful day; an early autumn day rather than a November one. The sea was a Mediterranean blue, the long line of the Lizard was pencil clear, a fishing boat with a red hull was passing Carn Barges, the heap of cliff rocks we stare out upon from Minack, and in the background from the direction of John Phillip's lovely old farm, I could hear the cackling of turkeys.

I fumbled with the catch of the gate.

'Ready, Jeannie?' I said, the others watching, 'take off his halter and let him go.'

Fred had never seen a donkey other than his mother. The gate opened and Merlin flashed by him, no pause for greeting or acknowledgement. I watched Fred's startled look as Merlin careered down the narrow path alongside the stable field, flinging up his hind legs like a bronco.

'Merlin,' I said, a little primly, 'is certainly boisterous.'

'He'll prove a match for Fred,' said one of his seconds, proudly.

Fred was astonished. He stood by the gate, ears pricked, motionless, watching in amazement the antics of only the second donkey he had ever seen in his life.

'Go on,' I said, trying to give him encouragement. 'Go on and join Merlin.'

'Yes,' said Jeannie, 'go and play!'

We let ourselves through the gate and we were now both pushing him. We have often pushed Fred one way or the other, and usually when a photograph is about to be taken and his bottom is facing the camera.

'Come on, Fred' I said, urgently, because I felt he was making a fool of himself in front of the others. 'Come on, show how beautiful you are.'

He *was* beautiful. At this time of year, with the thick winter growth of his brown coat, his fine head, and the

way he carried himself as he walked, he looked an aristocratic donkey, despite being denied an entry in the Stud
Book. Merlin looked shaggy compared with him.

'Merlin's on the way back!'

He dashed up to us, slithered to a stop, turned, and off
again, back legs flying, up through the gap into what we
call the Q.E.2 field. It is called the Q.E.2 field because
it was here that we stuck the pole of the washing line
into the ground, an orange table cloth attached to the
top of it in the form of a flag, when the then Captain of
the Q.E.2 brought the liner close inshore because of his
wish to see Minack. We stood there by the pole, Penny
and Fred beside us, while the liner's sirens blasted a
greeting . . . and the donkeys hooted in reply.

'He's not used to such space,' said Val Bailey.

It was now, after Merlin had disappeared through the
gap, that Fred began to move. He took a few steps,
paused, then took a few more until he reached the gap,
where he stopped, ears pricked again, bottom towards
us, staring . . . staring at this extraordinary sight of
Merlin racing round and round the field.

'They're going to be friends,' said Jeannie, hopefully.

'Not much sign of it yet,' I said.

'Let them be on their own,' said Jenifer. 'You'll see,
Merlin will settle down. He's the most lovable donkey I
have ever bred.'

'After you came to see him,' added Val, 'I didn't sleep
all night thinking of him going.'

There it was again, my sense of regret that he wasn't
an *unknown* donkey. Breeder and one-time owner living
comparatively close, and only natural they would be
thinking of him at Minack.

'Anyhow,' I said, jokingly, 'they haven't fought yet,
and we can much better see the situation after the week's
trial.'

'I'll come back then,' said Val, 'and I'll bring Des, my
husband.'

Periodically during the afternoon, Jeannie and I had a
look at the two of them; and that evening when I had gone

into the Lama field where we grow the Joseph Macleod daffodils, and Oliver was with me, I looked down on the stable field and, as the light died, watched them.

Fred was silhouetted against the darkening sea at the far end of the field, head down, grazing. Twenty yards away, Merlin too had his head down, grazing. In the distance, across the Bay, the Lizard Light flashed every few seconds.

I heard the sound of a curlew calling as I turned to go away, then another and another until, briefly, speeding west to the reeds of Marazion marshes or the mudbanks of Helford river, flew a concourse of curlews, the rush of their wings reminding me of a sudden gust of wind among trees.

I stood there listening for a moment and, when the sky was silent again, I went down the two steps from the field to the bridge, past the *escallonia*, and on down the path towards the barn. As I did so, a dark shadow dashed past me, then collapsed on the chippings a few yards in front of me. Oliver, tummy facing the darkening sky, was wanting attention again. I bent down and touched him with a finger, a token rub only, because I had no time to stop.

He came on beside me as I walked past the white seat on my left and the barn on my right, until I reached Monty's Leap, when a sudden cluck of a blackbird, startled in its roost in the brush beside us, stopped him for a moment, and he looked alert until he realised there was no danger. Oliver always tended to be on the alert at Monty's Leap. It was a leftover fear from the time when he was conducting his campaign to come and live at Minack. Monty's Leap in those days was the boundary line, and he knew that if he crossed it he would face the rage of Lama; or, though I do not like to remember this, the rage of myself who, anxious to protect Lama, would shoo Oliver away, shuffling my feet noisily on the chippings as I did so.

Oliver was born in a cave down the cliff. His mother was a small, wild, grey cat we called Daisy, and she was also the mother of Lama. Daisy, I believe, hoped that Lama would accept Oliver, the little black kitten, as a companion, but Lama would have nothing to do with him. Thereupon Daisy took the black kitten away from Minack and we did not see him again for four years when Oliver, as he was to be known, began to appear regularly on the other side of Monty's Leap. His courtship of us continued over two years, but Jeannie and I were always on guard because Lama was growing old, and we had no intention of upsetting her . . . Lama, who had come uninvited into our home after Monty died, the ginger cat we had brought from London.

A black cat, the double of Lama, courting us was strange enough, but a year after Oliver first appeared Ambrose arrived, and Ambrose was the outcome of a miracle performed by Oliver. I was standing beside Monty's Leap, Oliver a short distance away in front of me, when I heard a tiny miaow coming from the undergrowth to the right. A moment later, I had one of the strangest sights of my life . . . a tiny kitten, the colour of autumn bracken, the exact double of Monty as a kitten, stumbled from the undergrowth into the lane, whereupon Oliver rushed up to him and began licking him. It was the first of many times they were to show devotion to each other.

But now, as Oliver came along with me that November evening and we were crossing Monty's Leap, there was no discomfort to threaten him during the coming night, no rage for him to face. His aim had been achieved. He had become one of the cats of Minack; one of the cats who, over the four hundred years since the cottage was built, had sunned themselves on the boulders around the cottage, chased mice in the grass, climbed the trees and drank water at Monty's Leap.

I turned left through the gap into the field we call the greenhouse field because, although in this field we have a large part growing California daffodils, a small part growing White Lion, and another part growing our vegetables and fruit like raspberries, blackcurrants and gooseberries, the most important part, and most costly, is covered by four greenhouses each seventy feet long and twenty feet wide. From a distance they look impressive. They suggest prosperity. They give the impression that they belong to a grower who has no difficulty in deciding what to grow.

Such a decision was not difficult in the beginning. The greenhouses were mobile at the time, each one covering two plots, and we were full of enthusiasm and optimism. In summertime we grew tomatoes; in wintertime we moved the greenhouses over freesias, or chrysanthemums, or polyanthuses, or irises. We seemed to have created a pattern of growing which could go on for ever. We installed hot air heating and put in drip irrigation (long rubber lines with nozzles at intervals), and we firmly believed that we had secured a solid base on which financial survival was ensured.

I am not sure exactly when our hopes began to go awry. It was a gradual process, but perhaps the first sign was the day when one of the greenhouses, as we moved it from one plot to another, came off the rails. It was not a major incident at the time, because we soon moved it back to its proper position. It was, however, a warning that, after years of use, the rails of the greenhouse had gone out of alignment. First one greenhouse, then another, then another. All showed the same weakness, and as a result we stopped trying to use them as mobiles and used them as static greenhouses instead.

We changed, therefore, our pattern of growing. We continued to grow tomatoes direct into the soil but, for the winter crop, we used whalehide pots, laboriously filling them with earth, planting them with freesia corms, chrysanthemums and daffodil bulbs, and patiently watering them through the summer before carrying them from the space they occupied outside into the greenhouses as soon as we had lifted and taken away the now exhausted tomato plants.

We were absorbed in the work. We had paid help, in those days: someone to keep the routine moving when we might be otherwise engaged, but we were never just observers. We would spend hours at a time on our knees, picking the weeds from the whalehide pots which contained the freesias, and I would water them and water the chrysanths and the bulbs; dreamily dangling the hose along the rows of pots. I had no thought of writing in those days; nor did Jeannie. Our minds were in suspension. We were discovering the delights of being free from mental responsibilities, the delights of being manual workers, the extraordinary pleasures that can be obtained by those who do not have to make big decisions. Pick, pick, pick out the weeds. Hose this whalehide pot sufficiently, hose that one, hose this one. The relaxation of working without using our brains was ours.

Yet such an attitude on our part was a delusion. We were indulging ourselves as we picked out the weeds and watered the pots. We were only enjoying a respite from management. We still had to earn the money to pay the wages. We still had to pay for the pleasure of being our own masters, by taking risks, by finding the capital to pay for those risks. I remember a friend who had listened to my enthusiasm when I outlined my programme of erecting the greenhouses, who had listened as I described how my bank manager had allowed me a loan to buy them, but who still remained silent as I excitedly told him of the crops we were going to grow. His silence disappointed me. I was needing someone else's enthusiasm to bolster my confidence.

My friend's name was Joe Coward. He was a Midlands business man, who came on holiday with Dorothy his wife to Lamorna one year and, like many others before and after him, became infected with the wish to make the great change. More often than not, the infection only lasts during the length of the holiday and is cured by sensible thinking as soon as the holidaymaker returns home. But occasionally there are exceptions, and Joe Coward was one of them. He and Dorothy came to the conclusion that life in Lamorna would offer greater happiness than the routine life they were leading in the Midlands. They bought a plot of land on the hillside in Lamorna, built a small house, and set out to earn a living on a far lower scale than they had been used to.

Joe was a practical person. He had a piece of ground in the Lamorna valley where he grew violets for the market, and he also hired himself out as a casual farm worker. It was in this capacity that I first came to know him for, in potato harvest-time, we needed as much extra help as we could find, and Joe would come to Minack, carrying with him his personal long-handled Cornish shovel, and spend the day with us digging up potatoes. His role of farm worker, though so different from what he had been used to, suited him. He was a philosopher who liked to lean on the handle of his shovel, at the end of a row he had dug, staring out to sea, contemplating. He was around forty years old, had a slight squint, always wore a beret, was never without his terrier, Jefferson, liked to argue with me on any topic, and had a dry sense of humour. Jeannie and I were very fond of Joe.

In summertime, when the visitors came to Lamorna, he liked playing the part of a country character. He would stand at the bar in The Wink and regale them with local stories, or he would be in his garden which faced the lane going up to the cliffs, and call out some cheerful remark as a visitor passed by. There were always, of course, the standard remarks about the weather, but there was one remark, a piece of weather lore obtained by him from somewhere, which he made his speciality.

A couple of holidaymakers would pass by his garden, greetings would be exchanged, and one of the holidaymakers might say, looking up at the clear blue sky: 'Lovely day to be on holiday!'

Joe, too, would look up at the clear blue sky, pause a moment, then, without any intention of defusing the happiness of the holidaymakers, would remark: 'Don't be too sure!'

Naturally, such a remark caused puzzlement. Clear blue sky, a perfect summer's day, and yet a word of doubt from a local.

'Why?' was the inevitable question.

Joe now savoured the full flavour of his role as a country character. He would not reply immediately. He might bend down and pull up an imaginary weed, or turn to Jefferson and stroke him. Then, having created this minor tension, he would give his reason.

'The sun is burning,' he would say, smiling.

'How do you mean, "burning"?'

'We locals know when it is burning. The sun can be a balm, but it can also sting. When it stings, we call it burning, and it is burning today . . . and that means rain is on its way.'

I subscribe to Joe's theory. I am aware now when the sun is burning, and when this happens Jeannie and I will say to each other, or to anyone who might be with us: 'Joe's rain will be with us soon.' The forecast never fails.

He was helping us at the time when we were planning the greenhouses, and that was the occasion when he disappointed me. He was building a wall for us. There is an art in building a dry stone wall, and Joe, despite his background as a Midlands business man, was an expert at it. You have to have a 'feel' for stone to do this successfully, and Joe had this 'feel'; we have stone walls around Minack which will always be a memorial to him.

But he disappointed me that time when I needed encouragement. I believed that our boldness in borrowing the money to erect the greenhouses was the wisest deed we had done since we came to Minack, or I wanted to believe that. A wonderful period of growing prosperity seemed to stretch ahead of us. We had secured the base of our future.

Joe did not agree.

'You'll live to regret it,' he said.

'Why on earth do you think that, Joe?' I asked.

'They'll be white elephants.'

'What rubbish!'

He looked at me with a smile which was more of a laugh.

'Those pieces of ground now covered by all that expensive glass will make you worry what to grow in them. It will always have to be something special in order to get your money's worth out of the capital you have spent. But how would I look at that same ground?'

'Tell me.'

'No worry for me about getting my capital back, I

would just grow violets. A few pounds for the runners, and that's all I would have to think about.'

He was romancing a little, and I told him so.

'What about that frost two years ago,' I said, 'which turned your violet plants black?'

'Ah,' he replied, 'that cost me £5 of capital . . . what is it going to cost you if your precious greenhouse crop hits a glut market?'

We never lacked advice as to what to grow, or not to grow. The advisory officers of the Ministry of Agriculture were liberal with their help, and it was our fault that we treated them as oracles. This attitude was partly due to our upbringing. The parents of both of us belonged to the mould who, whenever a problem of any kind arose would say: 'Ask the advice of an expert.' It took me years to realise that experts are as fallible as the rest of us but, at the time I was listening to the words of advisory officers, my belief in infallibility still existed.

They were very useful, but I expected too much of them. I am inclined to expect too much of people. I am perpetually turning geese into swans; then I am surprised when whoever it is does not measure up to my expectations. There seems a persistent optimism in my nature which prevents my correcting this fault; and, in the case of the advisory officers, this persistent optimism resulted in my doing them a disservice. Their job was to advise, not to act as managers. It was my job to listen, weigh one piece of advice against another, then come to a decision. If it were the wrong decision, it was my responsibility, not theirs.

I ought to have realised, for instance, that I was only one of many growers they were advising; and so, when I poured out my problems, treating them as if they were father confessors, I should have known there were other growers behaving in the same fashion. These agricultural priests were, therefore, the recipients of a multitudinous number of growing secrets, and it was understandable that, without disclosing their sources, they made use of them. Thus, I might be told in general terms that Wedgwood iris made a lot of money the previous year, that it would be a good idea if I grew Wedgwood iris myself for the coming year . . . but my naïvety blinded me to the fact that every other grower who was seeking advice for their survival was receiving the same advice, and so a bonanza of Wedgwood iris would be grown everywhere —probably with glut results.

The advice of advisory officers is obviously much sought after on technical problems, for which these officers are largely dependent on their department's scientists. Much has been achieved by these scientists, many technical breakthroughs have been won, but there will be a backlash, the inevitable side effects of chemicals —or drugs.

It is several years since the publication of Rachel Carson's *The Silent Spring*, and its warning of the effects of modern technology on the land. It would be pleasant to believe that society had learnt a lesson from that book, but I doubt it. We are in such a hurry. We are caught up in the instant age. We want to see results without struggling to achieve them. And, because of this pressure, scientists are pushed to announce their startling discoveries before they have had time to give them long-term tests.

After three particular incidents, however, we said we would never trust scientific short-cuts again. One incident concerned a poison we once were advised to use against mice which were eating our anemone corms: spray a chemical on the ground, we were told, and the mice will disappear. What about any animal who might go over the same ground? 'Never thought of that,' was the answer. It is now banned.

The second incident concerns slug bait. It bewilders me that slug pellets are available everywhere, and that they are recommended because they are easier to use than a spray. Slug pellets, unless completely hidden from view, can kill a dog or a cat or a bird. They see the pellets on the ground, think it is food, and that is that. We know of two dogs who were killed in this way.

The third incident deals with the period when we were conscientiously looking after our daffodil bulbs, and we were advised to use certain chemical mixtures to protect the bulbs against the two scourges of bulb-fly and eel-worm. The bulb-fly chemical (which has also now joined the banned lists) was so powerful in its fumes that Jeannie went to bed for two days after we had used it; and the other chemical, the eel-worm chemical, was so poisonous that a friend of mine, who spilt a couple of drips in a puddle in his farm yard, found his ducks dying as a result.

Such incidents are very small ones in comparison with the vast number of technical short-cuts which are in use every day, and whose long-term effects we will never know until it is too late. The decision on the use of chemicals depends on the judgement of an elite few. The rest of us may bleat our intuitive warnings, but we have no evidence to back them up. Thus, we have to watch and wait. It is scaring to think, judging by past experience, how many chemicals or drugs which are in general use today (and officially safe) will be banned as dangerous within ten years.

Recently a hilarious document was issued by the Agricultural Departments and the Health and Safety Executive in this country . . . hilarious in the sense that only a macabre humorist in some concrete building could have written it. The document describes how the crops we consume are protected from weeds, fungi and insects, and the risks incurred by anyone who happens to be in the neighbourhood when the spraying takes place:

'The spraying season is here once again and farmers, growers, and aerial and ground contractors are reminded to take precautions to prevent spray drift. Drifting chemical spray, particularly weed-killers, can cause severe and expensive damage to neighbouring fields, nurseries and gardens. Spray drift may contaminate crops it is not intended to reach, may inconvenience or distress local residents and passers-by, and may put beneficial insects such as bees and ladybirds at risk. Remember, inconsiderate spraying can give farming a bad name.

'Before starting to spray, operators should check on weather conditions and should postpone spraying if they are unsuitable. Spraying should not take place if there is a risk of contaminating or damaging nearby susceptible crops, water supplies or fisheries. Pay careful attention to wind strength. Never spray in strong winds. During spraying, keep a careful watch for changes in wind strength and direction. If necessary, stop work until conditions improve. Remember to spray accurately, taking particular care near roads, public footpaths and residential areas. Make sure those in the field know what to do in the event of injury or accidents.

'Neighbouring farmers and other people close to the site should be warned in advance when spraying is expected to take place. They can, if they wish, take special precautions, such as keeping livestock and pets under cover and bringing washing indoors. Local beekeepers must be told of the expected dates and times of spraying at least 24 hours in advance if chemicals that are harmful to bees are to be used.'

So beware!

We had plenty of advice about our greenhouses besides that from the advisory officers. There was, for example, the Rosewarne Horticultural Station near Camborne, which does so much for Cornish growers, although it had, to our way of thinking, a drawback. One came away envious of their facilities, both financial and in manpower.

Near home, however, but a couple of miles away from us, was a greenhouse specialist called Peter. He came first to the district to be the greenhouse manager of a large estate but, soon after his arrival, the estate had to be sold. Thereupon Peter took over the greenhouse site himself. The estate was called Boskenna.

It was one of the loveliest estates in Cornwall, belonging

to the Paynter family, with deep woods going down to the sea; a family who owned various farms in the district and who, for many, many years, were the main source of employment in the St Buryan area. A too reliable source, in fact, because Boskenna was one of those old-fashioned estates where the squire was king and, although the squire might impose upon his workers the belief that they should touch their caps whenever he passed by, he, in his turn, considered it his duty to look after them in a paternal fashion, and this meant never to sack them. Thus, when the economics of the world changed, caps might still be touched . . . but the squire's pocket became emptier and emptier.

Colonel Paynter was the squire when we first knew Boskenna, and he was the man who on hearing that at last we were coming to live at Minack, said, looking at Jeannie: 'Is the casket worthy of the jewel?' He always wore a bowler hat and, one hot summer day, we accompanied him down to the Boskenna meadows where the new potatoes were being dug. The men and women who were working there belonged to families who had worked for generations at Boskenna, so the respect they showed to the Colonel in his bowler hat was imbued in them. But what amused me was the Colonel's attitude: he went slowly around each group, picking apples out of a bag he carried, and offering them in a benign way to each worker, as if he were offering a large bonus. It was a large bonus in a way. The Colonel was showing his appreciation.

Peter pulled down the old greenhouses of the estate and put up massive new ones. They were so vast that if you were standing at one end, you scarcely could recognise a face at the other end. I used to gape in wonderment when I visited them, and marvel at the long beds of roses, gerberas, stock, iris, chrysanthemums or whatever it was he was growing at the time. He gave the impression that he was in command of his growing, that the soil was sterilised regularly, the heat properly controlled, fertilisers available at the right time, water correctly applied . . . and, as a result, nothing ever went wrong. Our own efforts were so puny in comparison; so amateurish in contrast to such professionalism.

He had another interest, or hobby, an aviary of exotic birds which he built close to the greenhouses, breeding from them, exchanging them with other collectors. In both these spheres of interest, birds and greenhouses, he was always ready to help us. When Boris, our muscovy drake, was poisoned, it was to him we hurried to ask advice, and who consoled us when Boris died, saying that there was nothing we could have done to save him; and when, years later, Penny died, Peter made a special visit to see Jeannie, bringing her flowers, consoling her again over the inevitable feeling she might have done more. He had sometimes a bluff manner, a mask for his kind nature, but he had compassion, and an understanding of the basic values of life. As for his greenhouse knowledge, it was always at our disposal. He never fogged us with false expectations. Indeed, part of his character was to be a perpetual pessimist. Ever since I first knew him, he had the habit of foreseeing problems, real or imaginary; and when, one day shortly before Merlin arrived, I called on him, I found him at his most pessimistic.

'How are you getting on without Geoffrey?' he had begun by asking.

'Fine.'

Geoffrey, for several years, had been the mainstay for us at Minack. He left after wages and costs became so high that it was not economically possible to employ him.

'You're still managing everything on your own?'

We had twenty acres and seven thousand square feet of greenhouses. Several acres were growing daffodils.

'Yes,' I said, 'and it's such fun to be independent.'

'You're lucky.'

He was leaning against the door of one of his huge greenhouses.

'I was in Holland during the summer,' he went on, 'and you should just see the lines of production, just like car assembly lines, that they have set up for growing flowers and plants of every description. It is the same in Germany and other parts of Europe; and to beat the climate, these huge concerns have created vast growing areas in all parts of the world, flying their products to markets everywhere. They think in units of millions, and can therefore afford to take their profit margins in pennies. Their products are sold like tins of peas on a supermarket shelf. The small grower, the grower like myself, like you, can't hope to compete. That's the way everything is in this world. The small man simply can't cope.'

'It can't be as bad as all that for you,' I said. 'The quality of your flowers is talked about everywhere.'

'All right, maybe it is, but that doesn't count any more . . . one's fighting a losing battle all the time with expenses going up and prices going down.'

Peter, I realised, was exaggerating his problems. It was his customary pessimism. Yet if he, a professional, felt in this way, it would seem that amateurs like ourselves had no chance of survival. Computerised growing was certain to defeat us.

'It's a pleasant way of life,' I said, consolingly.

'Must be crazy to enjoy it,' he said, and I wasn't sure whether he was making a joke or was serious.

Independence always poses this problem. People the world over dream of giving up their regular jobs, saying goodbye to managers with whom they disagree, becoming free of the relentless routine of travelling to the office or factory, or of enduring the stress of pressures from those around them. It is a perennial dream for many. Yet, if the step to gain independence is taken, another vicious stress may take its place.

Jeannie and I have experienced that stress in the sense that, for long periods of time, we had scarcely the money to pay for the postage stamps on our letters, and we lived on scrags of meat and the vegetables we grew. Yet never for a moment did we ever discuss giving up and returning to the London circle which we had left. Why? Jeannie's perpetual optimism was one reason. Another was that we shared a desire to find values in life other than those to which we had become accustomed. Surface values are fun to enjoy in spurts, but to live with them permanently leads one into a disquieting vacuum. Life runs away and there is nothing to show.

The values we were looking for were those which help to achieve peace of mind and, in our case, they were composed both of negative and positive values. The negative values from which we wished to be freed included the weariness of being with people who mocked sincerity, people who relished intrigue, people who smiled to your face while planning to cheat you, people who considered simplicity a fault, people who were immune to other people's feelings . . . all ingredients of the rat race.

The positive values, on the other hand, which we set out to gain, are more difficult to define. One is in the position of a lover of Mozart, trying to explain the subtleties of a Mozart quartet. Many will be forever deaf to the subtleties. Many, and I was one, will slowly become aware of them just as I slowly became aware oı the multitude of subtleties that have enriched our life at Minack . . . like the evening when Oliver was with me and I watched Fred and Merlin, and he followed me down the lane to the greenhouse field.

As we reached the gap at the entrance of the greenhouse field, I flushed a wood-pigeon from a tree on my left and it flew away, bashing through the branches, and I momentarily thought how strange that the flight of a wood-pigeon through a wood should be so noisy, the flight of an owl so silent. I went into the first greenhouse and turned the handle which controlled the vents, closing them; then into the second greenhouse, the third, the fourth, shutting the sliding doors as I left them. A nightly routine, yet an unnecessary one. Nothing of importance was growing in the greenhouses. Nothing of commercial value. My only reason for opening the vents during the day was to air the soil. The greenhouses would be empty until the tomatoes were planted.

It was dark when I had completed my task; dark except for a glow of light from the windows of the cottage.

'Come on, Oliver,' I said, 'home.'

I had reached the end of the barn, where it is joined by a low stone wall which separates the lane from the stable field, when I saw a patch of white facing me, close to the wall. The white of a donkey nose. It was Merlin.

'Merlin,' I said, 'are you on your own? What have you done with Fred?'

I put out my hand and Merlin pushed his nose, soft like a warm cushion, into it.

'You're very friendly,' I said, flattered that so soon he was taking notice of me, 'but where's Fred?'

At that moment, from out of the darkness at the far end of the field, came the crescendo of a hee-haw.

'Fred!' I shouted, 'come and join us!'

No sign of him. The hee-haw died into silence and no shadow came out of the darkness. Fred was in a huff. He was not going to share me with Merlin.

THREE

I woke up next morning and listened drowsily to Oliver purring close beside me; and I thought of those people who throw their cats out at night whatever the weather, as my father and mother would have done had a cat dared to venture into my childhood home, as I myself would have done before I met Jeannie.

Oliver was small for a male cat (in due course he was neutered), and when we first saw him, indeed when our vet also first saw him, we thought he was a female. At that time, the beginning of the period when he took up his regular position on the far side of Monty's Leap, we were never able to get close enough to touch him. In retrospect, I realise that his extra-sensory cat powers had made him aware that Lama was coming to the end of her time and, before long, there would be a vacancy which he could fill; and so as the months passed, he became bolder.

I had first made him a little shelter in the undergrowth on the other side of the Leap and, after Ambrose arrived, I made them both a more permanent one in the tractor house. But, at the beginning of the winter that Lama died, Oliver began appearing at the door; and during a bitter cold spell, we allowed him to come into the porch at night and I collected the cardboard lid of a daffodil box and fixed it on the cane chair in such a way that he had protection against the cold; Ambrose too.

Ambrose, on the other hand, showed no sign of wishing to fill a vacancy. From the moment that he appeared with Oliver, as a kitten, he had been as nervous as a wild animal. We marvelled at the miracle that we once again had a kitten the colour of autumn bracken, the double of Monty, but he showed no sign of offering the affection Monty had given us from the beginning. He ran away even when we tried to lure him with a plate of fish or saucer of milk, and he only came to the shelter of the porch at night when there was no sign of us and Oliver had already arrived through the half-open window. Ambrose, in those days and nights, was as elusive as Tinkerbell, while Oliver was earnest and persistent, and took risks.

One night, for instance, a risk he took caused us distress. Lama had three favourite places where she liked to sleep. Sometimes it would be in the spare bedroom on the bed; sometimes on the wood top of the Heatstore by the window alongside my desk and sometimes, of course, on our bed. In her latter months she seemed to prefer to be on her own, and it was not often she joined us, but when she did we were pleased. I would wake up and find her in deep sleep beside me.

Once upon a time, she went in and out of the window during the night, but this we had stopped her from doing by fixing a wire frame across the open window. It was the same wire frame I had once used to stop Monty when, soon after his arrival from London, he had been chased by a fox during one of his nocturnal prowls. He had leapt through the window in terror on to the bed and, when I jumped to the window to see what had caused his terror, there beneath the window-sill, within hand-stretching distance, was the fox.

On this particular night when Oliver took a risk, a full moon was shining through the bedroom window which faces the sea, and the light of the moon lit the bedroom. In the early hours I woke up, felt with my hand the warm comfort of Lama lying beside me then, a minute or two later, saw another ball of black curled up at the bottom of the bed. I was appalled. For the first time, Oliver had come indoors. For the first time, he had gone to sleep on our bed. He had taken advantage of Lama's deep sleep . . . and of mine. He had jumped from the garden on to the window-sill and pushed the wire frame aside.

This rivalry between the two was sad, but inevitable; and shortly before Lama died, there was another incident which caused us distress.

It was a warm March morning, the Ascania violets were scenting by Monty's Leap and the daffodils were crowding the meadows and peering haphazardly from the hedges, and Lama, to our delight, suddenly wished to go for a stroll. She started off down the path towards the barn, purposefully, as if she knew exactly where she wanted to go, but when she reached the rock which sticks up out of the grey chippings close to where a car will park, a gust of a breeze pushed her off balance and she half staggered. She recovered herself and continued to walk, not very steadily, down the lane to Monty's Leap, where she paused, knowing she had not the strength to jump the little stream. I picked her up, very light, and put her down on the other side; and then Jeannie and I watched her turn left through the gap into the greenhouse field and, as we did so, we both suddenly realised what we were witnessing. This had been a regular route of hers for years and we were watching her do it for the last time.

She went across the stretch of grass, then turned left into the small orchard and, after pausing, after we had bent down and gently stroked her, she tottered on towards the cottage. At that moment, she saw the fallen branch of the willow tree which had always been a place where she liked to sharpen her claws; she did so again, and so firmly that we both were fleetingly duped by optimism. Then on again, up beside the Orlyt greenhouse, until she reached the patch of ground which is the rose garden. It was here that she suddenly saw Oliver.

He was sitting upright, black tail curled round to his

paws, the tip gently flicking, and there was an air of confidence about him that I had not noticed before. He no longer seemed to be the outsider trying to win favours. The impression he gave was that he at last belonged to Minack, and soon he would be the accepted inhabitant. Not yet, however, for I shooed him away . . . and, as I did so, I caught a look from Lama that I will not forget. She was envying him. She did not want to go. There, in front of her, was the successor to her happiness. Time ahead of him. Then I had an uncanny sense of another thought in her mind. 'One day,' she seemed to be thinking, 'you, Oliver, will be in the same situation.'

Two black cats and each of them had come uninvited to Minack. I, who from my childhood had always been superstitious about the good luck properties of a black cat, despite my dislike of the general cat fraternity, was having black cats thrust upon me. It was magic. It is an age when magic is unfashionable. Everything has to be analysed. Social Reports are endlessly issued by Government departments, institutes and societies, telling us how we behave, how an average percentage of us act in this way, another percentage in that, and we are conditioned into believing that the concept of reason is omnipotent. Yet, if one thinks about it, it is the magic of the unexplainable that will always rule our lives.

So here I was four years later, Lama remembered, but Oliver loved, drowsily listening to Oliver purring beside me; and as I lay there, I found my mind developing a pleasant sense of anticipation . . . the novelty of a new arrival, Merlin, down there in the stable field awaiting our attention. The question mark as to how Fred was reacting; the prospect of taking them both for a walk.

Jeannie was awake.

'Let's take the donkeys to the onion meadow before breakfast,' I said.

The onion meadow bordered the boundary between Minack and what I have called the Pentewan meadows. We once rented these meadows at a time when we innocently believed that by filling the meadows with seed potatoes we would become rich. It was very early land, so the potato crop would normally fetch a very good price. Unfortunately, the weather cycle changed as soon as we took over the meadows and, instead of the usual balmy springs, the weather was violent, either in the form of frost or gales, and we never collected the bonanza we expected. Indeed, each year we had miserable crops and lost money—and I also nearly lost my foot.

One day, one autumn day when I was rotovating a steep meadow with a formidable hand-controlled rotovator in preparation for the January planting of the potato seed, the rotovator hit a rock, turned over out of control and, as it did so, one of the curved tines caught my left foot, pierced it, and left me lying on the ground with the rotovator straddled across me. I might have lain there for a long time had it not been for my neighbour at that time, John Ellis. He was ploughing a field some distance away, but happened to be watching me, and saw the accident happen and rushed to my rescue. I was in bed for a fortnight.

When we were dressed, we went down to the stable meadow gate, picked up the two halters which I had left lying on the hedge, and called: 'Donkeys!'

There was, in fact, no need to call Merlin. Merlin came scampering towards us as soon as he saw us approaching, head down, back legs flying, with all the excitement of a puppy. He stood quietly as we opened the gate, then, just to be perverse, he turned and rushed away.

'He's *very* pretty,' said Jeannie.

There was a thick fringe on his head, thick enough to half cover his eyes, so that one felt one should brush it back if he was to see properly, as one does with an old English sheepdog. His coat was long and the texture soft and would need, I realised, much grooming. His legs, however, were the most surprising part of him because they were so stocky, not due to the bone structure but to the quantity of coat which covered them, resembling old-fashioned plus-fours and, to add to this strange appearance, was the contrast of his tiny hooves; hooves which reminded me of a ballet dancer's shoes compared with Fred's clodhoppers. He was a delight to look at, and I could understand how, young as he was, he had been a prize winner at various Shows: best foal at the Penzance Agricultural Show; best foal at the Devon County Show; sixth in the national 'Mare with Foal' class at the prestigious Stoneleigh Show. It concerned me that, with such a record, his Show days were over.

'I'll fetch a carrot,' I said. That age-old method of catching a donkey; and when I came back and called Merlin, he came with a rush and, to his annoyance, I held it dangling in front of his nose until the halter was firmly in place.

I had another carrot for Fred. I called him. He took no notice. Jeannie called. He lifted his head, looked across the grass at us, hesitated, then with me waving the carrot in the air, he slowly advanced.

'Hurry up, Fred, or Merlin will have it!'

This incident, this pastoral game with two donkeys, was of trivial importance in the context of the issues of today, such as the right of strikers to hold the public to ransom, or issues like the advantages and disadvantages of the European monetary system, or the intrigues among academics as to whether this poet or that should fill the Poetry Chair at Oxford, or whether ITV ratings will be higher on Christmas Day than the BBC's, or whether the Soviet Union and America have enough warheads to blow each other up. Such issues are of public concern, but as all issues are relative to the situation in which they are involved, the question as to whether Fred would cross the stable field and partake of the carrot before Merlin seized it for himself was the issue in our isolated setting that momentarily dominated *us*.

Fred had his carrot and, as he munched, I put on his halter and then off we all went towards the onion meadow, Jeannie leading Merlin. I have never learnt why it is called the onion meadow though, naturally, I have presumed that onions were once grown there. We have never tried to grow anything in the meadow. The soil is too shallow, and only grass, poor grass, grows in it; though it is grass which Fred and, once upon a time, Penny, have always enjoyed. It was, in fact, a good place to leave the donkeys; and if Merlin behaved during the week's trial, he too, would find himself eating the grass of the onion meadow. The reason was this. Once the green spears of the daffodils were shooting above the ground, the donkeys could not be in the daffodil meadows. They would, therefore, be confined to the stable meadow and the big field above the cottage garden. Such an area would be like a palace garden for most donkeys, but we had found, during the Fred and Penny days, that donkeys, like many human beings, always expect more than they have got. Hence in daffodil time our donkeys, as a change, roamed the grass of the onion meadow.

In order to reach the onion meadow, we have to walk for a hundred yards or more along the national coastal path; the admirable path which edges the coast of England, Wales and Scotland. On either side of the path are daffodil meadows, four of them in fact, and in these daffodil meadows, during non-daffodil times, the donkeys munch. However, in order to stop them from breaking out, I temporarily place a galvanised bar across the coastal path at the gap where we turn right after passing through the white gate at the bottom of the stable meadow, and when I put up the bar, I leave the halters in obvious sight, as a sign that the bar is for a purpose other than to hinder someone from walking along the path.

One summer this bar, along with a shorter one which I use as a supplementary form of defence, was the centre of a curious sequence of incidents.

The first took place on a hot July day some time in the late afternoon, though I was not aware of it until the evening when I went for a stroll. The donkeys, Fred and Penny at the time, had spent the day in the big field above the cottage. At this period of the year, when walkers are often on the move along the coastal path, we let the donkeys roam the daffodil meadows only in the early morning and, by eleven o'clock, we have brought them back to Minack. We adopted this routine because we did not want to embarrass any walker by the attention he might otherwise receive from the donkeys. Walkers often carry packs on their backs and these packs are an irresistible bait to the donkeys. On occasions I have seen a walker hurrying along the path, faster and faster, fearfully glancing behind him, while one of the donkeys, Fred most likely, kept pace. It was not the walker who was threatened; it was the pack.

I went for a stroll on that particular evening and was surprised to find the galvanised bar firmly fixed in its anti-donkey position across the path, despite the fact that the donkeys had not been in the meadows all day. The sight irritated me and I blamed it on a passing holiday-maker's prank; and it especially irritated me because the bar might have suggested that I was deliberately blocking the path.

I thought no more of it until a few days later, the donkeys once again having been absent from the meadows, the bar was once again across the path; then a few days later again, and a couple of days later once again. Clearly my original idea that it had been the work of a passing holidaymaker was wrong and, though a holidaymaker was still the most likely culprit, it would have to be a holidaymaker who was staying in the district. One wondered also as to why he had chosen to play such a strange game. Had the donkeys been in the meadows behind the bar, there might have been a warped reason why someone might have *removed* the bar in order to let the donkeys escape. A few years before, for instance, itinerant potato pickers who were working in the area used to amuse themselves by opening the stable meadow gate and letting the donkeys loose on the cliffs. Their aggro gesture might be understood . . . but this was someone putting *up* the bar when the donkeys were *not* there.

We proceeded to keep a look out, making sudden visits to the spot, and sometimes we would find the bar untouched, and at other times we would find the bar once again across the path. I got up in the early morning; went to have a look late at night. I hovered with field glasses on the other side of the valley like a detective on watch, but still I never caught sight of anyone touching the bar. All through July, then three weeks into August. No pattern to the act that I could discover. Three or four days without anything happening, then again the bar would be across the path; or sometimes the interval would be only a day.

The climax of this mysterious sequence of events took place on a Friday in the third week of August and, to this day, is inexplicable. Jeannie, being influenced by being half-Scot, half-Irish and living in Cornwall, likes to believe in the existence of pixies, leprechauns . . . and Hobberdy. Hobberdy, you may remember, is the imp which K. M. Briggs in his book describes as the imp who lives in old houses, takes care of the owners, and who enjoys displaying his sense of humour by performing extraordinary antics. Thus, when we lost a pair of silver salad ladles, then found them beautifully polished under the bird table six months later, Jeannie attributed the mystery to Hobberdy's form of humour. So, also, when I lost my wrist-watch and found it a couple of days later on top of the Orlyt greenhouse roof. And, too, when Jeannie carefully packed one of her drawings in a parcel, despatched it to a friend . . . then received a package back from the friend containing a cat's comb. The comb had been found by the friend in the carefully packed parcel . . . it had been lost at Minack three years before. So it was that when the final, and most peculiar of the bar incidents took place, Jeannie conveniently blamed it on Hobberdy.

To fix the bar in a firm position, I had to heave up a heavy piece of granite rock so that its weight dwelt on one end of the bar. It required an effort on my part to put it into place and, for someone like Jeannie, it was far too heavy to lift. I certainly did not have the strength myself to carry it more than a few feet.

However, on this August Friday, the actual day after which the bar was never put across the path again, I found the rock had disappeared. My first reaction was that it had been pushed away into the undergrowth which, at that time of the year, became rampant. I searched in ever-widening circles and there was not a sign of it. Months later, when winter gales had broken the undergrowth down to grass level, I searched again, thinking that it might have been carried some distance before it was dropped. I have never found it, and I have no clue as to what happened to it.

On the way to the onion meadow, I took off Fred's halter and he wandered ahead of us on the path, pausing, pushing his head into the hedge, nibbling the tip of a bramble, which he proceeded to consume as if it were a long strand of spaghetti. A solemn, reliable Fred. Merlin, on the other hand, was alert. His head was turning this way and that, inquisitive as a child in a new playground, and he was straining at the halter so that Jeannie was having difficulty in holding him.

'Better let him off,' I said.

'He's excited. We don't want anything to go wrong.'

'He can't run away.'

'Stop it, Merlin . . . Merlin, stop it . . . I can't hold him!'

I shot out my hand to catch the rope lead from the halter as it slipped from Jeannie's hand, but I was too late. Free! He couldn't believe it . . . and he was off, racing along the path, past Fred, who took no notice, up the slight hill and out of sight.

'He'll trip on the rope!'

The rope, dangling from the halter, was a danger. Many times in the past Fred or Penny had gone off with the halter still over their heads and the rope dangling and it had caused us to laugh. They would be walking away from us and would step on the rope, then wonder why they could not move. A situation in which one could genuinely call a donkey an ass.

But Merlin racing away at speed was a different matter.

'Supposing he tries to jump the stile into the Pentewan meadows,' said Jeannie, as we hastened forward, 'and he trips on the rope . . . he could break his neck!'

'Don't panic,' I said.

'Panic or not . . . hurry!'

We ran up the slope and soon reached the gap leading into the onion meadow and found the meadow empty. It is a beautifully situated meadow, a meadow which would send a property developer into ecstasies if there were not a ban on building on our coast . . . facing the sea, the Wolf Rock Lighthouse in sight to the west, the curve of the Lizard to the east, fishing boats passing, merchant ships on the horizon.

'Where has he disappeared to?'

'I can't guess,' said Jeannie.

I ran down to the stile which divided the onion meadow from the Pentewan meadows and, when I reached it, I called out:

'No sign of donkey feet here.'

So where was he?

We were calling out: 'Merlin! Merlin!'

But, instead of Merlin, Fred lumbered into view. Once upon a time, Fred was as elusive as Merlin was proving to be. He then was the new one, trotting along beside Penny his mother, experiencing the same new discoveries that were exciting Merlin. In those days there was no stile between Minack and the Pentewan meadows, and Penny would race Fred at great speed across what is known as the 'thirty-lace' meadow, then along through the dairyman's meadow, past the Pink Hut where we used to 'shoot' our potato seed (and where we once housed a sick badger), then up past the quarry. By now they would be out of sight of us, until finally we'd catch up with them standing outside the three cottages, in one of which Jane, the heroine of *A Drake at the Door*, used to live. Fred, no older than Merlin, loved these races; and there is a photograph of me standing beside him outside Jane's cottage. Jeannie took it. We had caught up with him after one of the races, and I am standing there with Fred, captured by the halter, alongside me, and a vista behind us of the rugged coast with the Logan Rock in the distance.

'Merlin! Merlin!'

A gull went crying overhead, as if in answer.

'There's only one place left he could have got to,' said Jeannie.

'I know . . . he's gone down the cliff.'

We have two cliffs and they are separated by a mass of elders and blackthorn, so each is reached by a different route. They are not, strictly speaking, cliffs at all. They are steep slopes falling down to the sea, and one is called the Minack cliff, and the other has always been known as the onion cliff because it slopes down below the onion meadow. Each of these cliffs has tiny meadows, or quillets, cut into them so that they resemble giant steps going down to the rocks and the sea. The meadows of the onion cliff have been there for generations, but the Minack meadows were our own creation. We slashed them out of the undergrowth, hacking at the roots in the ground and turning the soil with the long-handled Cornish shovel.

These were long-ago days. Growing potatoes in cliff land is history now. Nobody can afford the hand labour that is required. The land used to be turned by shovel in the late autumn, planted with seed in late January and February, kept hoed during subsequent weeks, and then in May there started the harvesting of the crop. It was a laborious job digging the rows, filling the baskets and slowly carrying them up the cliff and weighing them at the top. Yet there was deep satisfaction in the work. The baskets, or chips as they were locally called, used to be lined with the leaves of the potato plant. Each potato was carefully placed in the chip and, at the end of the day, someone would remark: 'They're a fine lot of samples.' Samples was always the word which was used when there was a summing up of a potato crop.

But a sense of pride in your work, although providing you with basic satisfaction, will not earn a living if outward circumstances are against you. Thus, when sophisticated potato harvesters became increasingly efficient, it was inevitable that the humble potato could no longer be treated with the care you would give an orchid. And so, the carefully packed chips, the fine samples, went into history.

We planted daffodil bulbs instead. We planted Magnificence, Joseph Macleod and California in the Minack cliff, and Magnificence in the onion cliff. The pundits advise that daffodil bulbs should be dug every three years, then sterilised, separated and planted again in new ground. This, no doubt, is the course everyone *should* adopt, but again the question of time and cost complicated the situation. Such advice simply cannot be followed in the cliff. Once in the ground, the bulbs have to be left there. The big growers, with their huge mechanical investment, can follow the pundits' advice, but the cliff workers have to cross their fingers and hope their bulbs will survive. It is extraordinary how they do. We have had bulbs in the same meadows for ten years and more and they continue to bloom. In some years, and in certain varieties, there will be poor crops; but then, when I have consulted one of the big growers who has obeyed every rule in the book, he will tell me that his daffodil crop is also light. Nature still seems to control both the cliff and the pampered fields.

Down the cliff . . . somewhere down there, was Merlin. The path that leads to it cuts through shoulder-high

44

blackthorn and brambles and, by late summer, the path itself is obscured by bracken. In the autumn it is my job to open up the path and also the meadows which, by this time, are similarly dense with bracken. Once upon a time, it was a long, laborious task, performed with the old-fashioned Father Time scythe; pleasant to perform in one's imagination, but back-breaking and very slow. One day, however, I acquired a Japanese machine called a Brush Cutter, which has revolutionised much of my labouring work. Slung across my back, driven by a noisy, powerful miniature engine, the circular cutter blade (or a nylon string in certain circumstances) is at the end of a five-foot bar, which I hold with my hands and which I sweep to and fro, just as I would have done with the Father Time scythe. It slices through the bracken and all other undergrowth obstacles and, when I change over to the part which operates the nylon string, it has another advantage. You cannot go too near rocks with the blade for fear of damaging it, but you can steer the nylon string as close as you like. Indeed, I now use it delicately on the weeds that grow up around the glass at the base of the greenhouses.

'Merlin! Merlin!'

We had come to the steep section of the path and, for a second, I was irritated by the sight of a torn blue polythene fertiliser bag blown from some neighbouring field on to a gorse bush, then a red one hanging limply on a black-thorn; examples of untidy modern farming, and I made a mental note that later I would pick them up. We hurried on and soon reached the first of the meadows where grow the Magnificence daffodils. No sign of Merlin.

'He must be at the bottom,' said Jeannie, from behind me.

The bottom meadows were some fifty yards from the rocks, the blue elvan rocks which edge the sea, and there was undergrowth in between; and so, unless Merlin had gone berserk, he could not have made a way through the undergrowth to the rocks. Yet, I was apprehensive.

We had turned the first corner and had begun the

descent to the bottom when both of us, simultaneously, gave a shout.

'Merlin!'

He took no notice. He was standing halfway down the cliff, sideways to the path, ears pricked, back arched, looking a worthy reminder of his Show championship days. He was quivering with excitement.

A mile off-shore, the white painted *Scillonian* was sailing by on her way to the Scilly Islands.

Merlin had seen his first ship.

From that moment, the onion cliff became the Merlin cliff.

FOUR

'A menacing date is looming up,' I said.

'We talked it over ... you thought you ought to accept.'

'So long ago, February when the invitation came, I couldn't visualise that December the ninth would ever arrive.'

'Still ten days to go.'

It was a date to speak in Manchester.

'I wish I could find an excuse to get out of it,' I said.

'You can't, so stop worrying. Anyhow, you said the chief reason you had for accepting it was your nostalgia for Manchester.'

'Yes. It gave me two of the happpiest years of my life.'

'Concentrate your mind on that, then,' said Jeannie, in practical fashion.

I am perpetually aware of the conflicts within myself. I have been aware of them ever since I drew away from the conventional standards of my youth ('Always be nice to servants in other people's houses' being the astonishing advice of my housemaster when I left Harrow), and I was helped by reading writers who had *involved* themselves in living full lives. I found no comfort in academic writers and philosophers; no inspiration from intellectual theories as to how youth should struggle for fulfilment, or how youth should attain experience. Thus, only writers who portrayed the realities of life, the subtle tensions which seem so often to be in opposition, who wrote about characters with whom I could identify one of my selves, writers who seemed to reflect my hopes and fears, who suddenly flashed light into a corner of my mind . . . only writers such as these fascinated me; and, of these, two stood high above all the others, Marcel Proust and Somerset Maugham.

My young life was so predictable, so inhibited by ropes of conventional thinking that I was conditioned into believing that life was a straight road of good or evil, of good manners or bad. There were no side roads, no alley-ways. Everyone was judged by their outward behaviour and, if they did not measure up to their expected behaviour, they were shunned. No allowance was given for inner conflicts. No forgiveness offered to those who strayed into an alleyway.

I sensed this attitude was wrong, but I found no Svengali to enlighten me. This is not entirely true. My problem was that when I did meet a potential Svengali, whether it was a man or a girl, I was tongue-tied. My inhibitions blocked any ease of manner on my part, so I gave the impression of disinterest to the person concerned; and though an effort might be made to loosen me up, I would fail to respond. A devil within denied me the opportunity I craved for.

I, therefore, felt safe only with writers. They became my absentee Svengalis. I was able to read their works without fear of being sabotaged by my inhibitions and, in reading Proust and Maugham, I discovered, naïve though it may sound, that other people had doubts and expectations like my own and could be confused and behave foolishly. This course of self-inquiry, however, still left me in my hidebound environment and, though I was beginning to learn that even such an environment can be enriched if you develop an inward instead of a

48

materialistic outlook, I felt as if I were in chains. This is why, as Jeannie said, I had this nostalgia for Manchester. Manchester was to release me from my chains.

For the next few days after the episode of the onion cliff, Merlin behaved gently. He welcomed our attention; allowed us to place his halter on him by pushing his head forward and thus making it easy for us to do so and, most important of all, treating Fred with respect. I could not say they were friendly in the way I would have wished, but there was no sign of conflict. They were two donkeys who were tolerating each other, in the way that two human beings might behave if circumstances had forced them together.

Then, on the day before his week's trial was up, when we were expecting Val Bailey and her husband to arrive and hear our verdict, Merlin performed an extraordinary feat.

Two children walked down the winding lane with their mother, hoping to see Fred, but knowing nothing of Merlin. I was not there to see them arrive because I had walked up to the well to check whether the water pump was working. Recently, it had been behaving erratically (our well is thirty yards from the cottage, strangely on top of the hill, is thirty feet deep, provides only five minutes pumping per day in late summer and autumn, but has water of the quality of a mountain spring). On this occasion, it was not the well which was failing to give us a supply . . . it was the pump.

I had just reached the well when I heard a distant shout: 'Help!' It puzzled me. It did not sound like Jeannie, nor did it have the note of distress. It was more like a cry of laughter, as if a child had been cornered in a predicament which was causing much amusement.

I ran back past the cottage and down towards the barn, and there I saw Merlin, his back towards me, his nose among the wallflower plants which lined the little flower bed beside the barn. At the same time, I saw the young mother and the two children.

'What's happened?' I said, a little crossly. My first

thought had been that they had not walked the straight-forward way down the lane, but had come up from the cliff path through the gate and left the gate open.

The children, two little girls, were in peals of laughter, as if they were laughing at a clown in a circus.

I saw now that the gate was shut.

'What's happened?' I said again.

'We were only talking to him,' said the mother, nervously.

'But he's outside when he should be in the field.'

'He jumped out,' said the mother.

'Jumped out?' I exclaimed. 'How on earth did he do that?'

I realised that the mother did not think the incident as funny as did her children. She was scared.

'He jumped from that bank by the gate!'

The bank, a form of wall, was five feet high.

'Golly,' I said, restraining my language, 'he might have broken his legs.'

'We were only just talking to him . . .'

'It's not your fault.'

'Susan was holding out her hand . . . then he suddenly leapt and nearly knocked us over.'

'You *must* have been frightened.'

'I was, but not the children.'

The children, doubtless because of my arrival, were now solemn, but I guessed it would not take long to get them laughing again.

'Children,' I said, 'we've got a job to do. You have to help me catch Merlin.'

Merlin had left the wallflower bed, had moved to the centre of the lane, thrown up his back legs in a gesture of high excitement, and set off for Monty's Leap. The situation was critical. Once across the Leap, he could race up the lane, up the hill, past the farm buildings, and on and on to the main road. (It has always been one of my nightmares that the donkeys might escape in this way.) The only chance we had was to cut him off by the gap into the greenhouse field. It would have been useless for me to follow him. He would only have hastened away faster.

At this moment, Jeannie appeared from round the corner of the cottage.

'Jeannie,' I cried, 'Merlin's out!'

She dropped the saucepan with the kitchen debris she was taking to the dustbin.

'What do you want me to do?'

'If you dash round through the orchard you may cut him off. I'll stay here to catch him if he gallops back.'

It was asking a lot of her. She had to dash fifty yards through the orchard, past Lama's grave, into the greenhouse field, then right for another thirty yards to the lane.

Then I turned to the children.

'You and your mother,' I said, 'must stand just there, between the white seat and that rock and so, if Merlin turns back and starts racing up towards the cottage, you'll be blocking his way and then he'll turn left through the gate which I am now going to open.'

I did so.

'Children,' I said firmly, and they were relishing the situation, 'jump up and down if Merlin comes towards you and shout: "Go into the stable field, Merlin!" '

Jeannie cut him off. She reached the Leap before he crossed it, while he was tasting the leaves of the heliotrope which lines the side of the lane. His delight in these leaves, which he had never tasted before, had given us the chance. He saw Jeannie, realised he was trapped, kicked his back legs into the air again, and rushed back towards me, the two children and their mother. We were a solid wall. Merlin had to surrender. There was nothing he could do but rush past us with a final flourish of his back legs, then carry on through the gate and join Fred.

Fred until then had been absent, remaining in another part of the field, disdaining any interest in Merlin's antics. But when Merlin at last returned, Fred came measuredly across the field and up to him. It was as if he were talking to him. It was as if he were telling Merlin not to be a fool. Jumping from a five-feet-high bank was dangerous. Fred did not want to lose Merlin. Fred did not want to hoot on his own again.

Thus, when Val and Des Bailey, the couple from Skinners Bottom, arrived the following day, I was able to tell them that Merlin had passed the test; that Fred had accepted him. It was not news, I felt, which they accepted joyfully, and I sensed the reasons. They were being forced to sell Merlin because Merlin was too boisterous to be a suitable companion for their old donkey, but they loved Merlin and I felt, as they greeted me, that they were half-hoping I would tell them the week's trial had been a failure.

They were an interesting couple. Val was a nurse in a London hospital when she met Des, a Jamaican, who had come to Britain to train as an anaesthetic technician. They married, became dissatisfied with London life and, in due course, he resigned from a tutorial post and the two of them set off for Cornwall. Des then gave up his original career and began a new one, a strange one in view of his past experience. He proceeded to teach himself to be a farrier. He sought advice from professional farriers, studied the movements of horses, how they stood and where the stresses were absorbed and, after a lengthy period, passed the entry examination of The Worshipful Company of Farriers. He is now a travelling farrier and his skill is well known in Cornwall.

Our own farrier is Kenny Mayle of St Buryan and he has looked after Fred's feet since Fred was born. His smithy at St Buryan, where he works with his brother Gerald and his bearded nephew Trevor, famous for his wrought-iron work, is a barn of a place; and though there are always metals of various shapes and sizes, machinery of every kind, all waiting for Mayle attention, the smithy is so large that it never appears crowded. Every three months we visit the smithy.

'Kenny,' we ask, 'can you come down and do the donkeys' feet?'

It is a chore for him to leave the smithy. We are asking a favour.

'Saturday morning . . . if it's fine, I'll be there.'

And, if the morning is wet, we have to wait another week, sometimes yet another.

A donkey's reaction to its feet being pared can vary. Sometimes Penny and Fred had behaved like broncos in a Calgary stampede, and Kenny would curse them and risk injury as he tried to seize a leg. So how, when the time came, would Merlin behave?

'Merlin,' said Des, before he left us, 'is as gentle as a lamb. He always stands quite still. No trouble at all.'

The question, however, as to whether Merlin would be as gentle as a lamb when a stranger attended his feet, did not for the moment arise. His feet were in prize condition. They were small and delicate compared with Fred's. They looked even too small and delicate, as if they were incapable of supporting him and, as the days went by, there was confirmation that this was so. He trotted prettily enough on level ground but, when he began rushing around the fields, especially if they were wet, he would slide here, slide there, like a Mini that is out of control. Fred never behaved so foolishly. Fred's feet were as solid as the tyres of a juggernaut lorry.

My menacing date, my date to speak in Manchester in the theatre in the basement below the Public Library, was now four days away. I hate public speaking, and I believe in the dictum of A. P. Herbert, who said that authors should be read but not heard. I prefer to stay at home. However, on this occasion, there was a difference. I had this nostalgia for Manchester. I had an absurd wish, for instance, to see again a pillar in the French Restaurant of the Midland Hotel, beside which I once had an after-theatre supper party many years ago.

So, although I was fearing the speech, I was becoming increasingly curious as to how I would feel when I saw again the places which would reflect the education of my youth. The only question which worried me was how Fred and Merlin, Oliver and Ambrose, and the gulls and Charlie the chaffinch would react in our absence. Always before we had Geoffrey to take charge and be at Minack during the day. This time, there would only be someone in the morning and evening to see that they were fed.

Fortunately, the someone was Margaret. At the end of

our lane by the main road is Tregurnow Pottery, which was begun several years ago by Margaret and George Smith; George was for a while a London taxi driver. The standard of the pottery they design and produce is of a collector's quality and, because they are their own team, their output is exclusive. However, there are periods of the year when their work is seasonally slack, and one of these periods, fortunately for us, coincides with the daffodil season. Then Margaret comes to help us and, because the three of us are on the same wavelength, the time is always a happy one, even when the prices are bad. She also, although the occasions were rare, was ready to watch over Minack when we were away and, although it was only a question of a morning and evening visit, we could feel reassured. If anything seriously went wrong, Margaret would deal with it.

Even so, I have neurotic fears when I leave Minack and I fuss foolishly. On this occasion, on the day before we set off for Manchester, an incident took place which added to the neurotic fears I already possessed. It concerned Oliver, Merlin and a blackbird.

There had been an influx of blackbirds into the area that November and, although an invasion is normal in any year, there were many more than usual. Ornithologists explain that they sweep across the Channel from Germany, Sweden, Norway and other European countries, then make their way south. A few will stay in the west for the winter before returning to their nesting haunts in the spring, but most of them will fly on to Southern Ireland and even to Spain. Thus, at the time we were about to leave, Minack was still host to a plethora of Common Market blackbirds, who were roosting at night in the wood and in the privet and *escallonia* hedges and were hungrily rushing around by day searching for earthworms and insects and pecking at fallen apples in the orchard.

Their activities intrigued Merlin. He soon began to believe that they were there for his entertainment and, when spying a blackbird poking his yellow beak into a tuft of grass a short distance away, he would proceed to stalk it, head down, in the manner of a hound following a scent. Needless to say, the blackbird would fly away long before Merlin came near him, but this did not deter Merlin from playing this game again and again. It was funny to watch him, enjoying a diversion to his day.

This particular day, however, he confused Oliver with a blackbird, or perhaps I am being too charitable. Perhaps he knew all the time that the black spot at the far end of the stable meadow was Oliver, sitting intent at the entrance to a rabbit hole, his back to the cottage, oblivious of all activity behind him, oblivious to the expanse of meadow across which Merlin was to proceed to stalk him.

We had left Fred and Merlin that morning in what we call the Q.E.2 field, which is on a higher level than the stable meadow so that, when standing in the Q.E.2 field, you can look down and observe what is going on in the stable meadow. It was from here that Merlin caught sight of Oliver crouching by the rabbit hole, a black spot resembling a blackbird.

It was the *Scillonian* on the way to the Scillies which alerted me as to what was happening. I was weeding the bank which runs alongside the stream to Monty's Leap, when I looked up because I heard the hum of the *Scillonian*. It is a habit for us to watch the *Scillonian* as she passes our section of the coast. There she is, white and proud, sailing sometimes in appalling weather, the one sea link between the islands and the mainland and, in doing so, one gains a form of reassurance; the *Scillonian* is sailing, life is normal.

I looked up and saw Merlin pass through the gap at the cottage end of the Q.E.2 field, cross the path and then into the stable meadow. At the same time, I saw the black spot beside the hedge below where we have the reservoir and, momentarily, I thought it was a question of here we go again, Merlin is chasing a blackbird. Then I realised that the black spot was not a blackbird, but Oliver; and Oliver was remaining motionless, his mind concentrated on the rabbit hole while Merlin came nearer and nearer.

One likes to be tolerant of the way a donkey treats another animal. Lama, for instance, used to rub herself against Penny's leg without Penny taking any notice. Birds, like jackdaws and magpies, will perch on the back of a donkey and it will display no objection. On the other hand, I have seen Fred so enraged by the barks of a dog that he has gone on to the attack, advancing on the dog as if he were bouncing, his two front feet going up and down, as if he intended to crush the dog if he reached him. On the rare occasions I have seen Fred behave in this way, I have not blamed him. Anyone has a breaking point when baited. I blame the dog owners who allow their dogs to wander the countryside uncontrolled.

Oliver, like Lama, was a trusting cat and he too would be prepared to rub the leg of a donkey. This trusting quality was, in fact, a fault. If a car came down the lane and he was lying in the middle of it, he would never think he was in danger. But this is one of the sad aspects of the cat world. They have no road sense. It seems that cats have never, in their attitude towards moving vehicles, grown out of the horse and buggy age. Progress has stood still for the cat fraternity.

Suddenly, I saw that Merlin was within a few yards of Oliver, and Oliver was still oblivious of what was happening; still his mind concentrating on the hope that a victim would soon appear from the rabbit hole.

'Oliver!' I thereupon shouted.

He turned his head.

'Oliver! Look out!'

He saw Merlin. The hoped-for victim was forgotten. He was over the hedge and away.

A near escape, but was it really a near escape? Surely Merlin was only having fun, and Oliver would have sensed his presence without my need to shout.

But, at the time, because we were about to leave for Manchester, I was alarmed. Here was another neurotic fear. Supposing Merlin *did*, while we were away, treat Oliver or Ambrose as a blackbird to chase? Margaret would be feeding them morning and evening, but what might happen during the rest of the time when they would be on their own?

Such imaginary fears are not unusual.

I have yet to meet a cat lover on holiday who is not worrying about the cat left at home.

FIVE

On Monday I was sitting in the corner of the sofa with Oliver on my lap.

On Friday evening I was again sitting in the corner of the sofa with Oliver on my lap.

'All over,' said Jeannie.

'Except the inquest as to how it went,' I said.

'We'll talk about it for weeks, I expect.'

I had enjoyed my nostalgic indulgence. Nostalgia, and sentiment for that matter, are treated with disdain by some. I do not understand why. Since we live in an era of violence and vandalism, of mass destruction capability and dwindling energy supplies, and of unthinking viewing, I think those who can indulge in a little nostalgia and sentiment are lucky people. It means they have memories of pleasure to balance against the problems of today.

My nostalgia for Manchester was born on a wet Sunday night when I arrived to begin my month's trial on the northern *Daily Express* and, on that night, I wrote in my diary:

'I trundled around in the rain looking for rooms until I finally came to Number 10 Ackers Street, where I am paying £1 a week. They are very forlorn, but the best I could find. They are theatrical digs (Ackers Street is full of theatrical digs) and I can only stay for a week because a Cochran Show is coming, and so I'll have to look for somewhere else.

'But tomorrow I start my new career. Curiously,

I don't feel so desperately lonely or unhappy. Perhaps tomorrow it will come over me. What a chance I have!'

The chance led me next morning to the *Daily Express* building in Ancoats Street and, from the moment I entered the building, I felt freed at last from my sheltered life as a clerk in Unilever by day and a Deb's Delight by night. I had entered another world, where people had a gusto for living, by-passing conventional niceties, where people did not adopt superior attitudes when faced by the frailties of their fellows.

That first morning the news editor told me to accompany a reporter to the Town Hall and to watch how he worked. I waited nervously in the reporters' room for my tutor (Guy Morgan, who became a famous film-script writer) to arrive; then followed him down the staircase with its (for me) sweet smell of printers' ink, and into the street. It was eleven o'clock in the morning. 'The pub is open,' were his first words to me, leading me across the street to the Land O'Cakes. 'We'll have a beer before we start work.' I had never been in a pub before.

I was, however, going to spend much time in the Land O'Cakes in the two years to come and, within its environment, I was going to experience the magic of friendship. No envy, a wish always to help and the blissful pleasure of being instinctively understood instead of laboriously having to explain. My colleagues did not pretend to be intellectuals; none of them ever had the chance to become academics and so, in the context of today's required qualifications, they were not equipped to reflect the mood of the people. But they were daily in touch with reality and this gave them compassion unencumbered by man-made theories as to what was fair or unfair. They were on the side of feeling in the eternal fight, as Jean Renoir described it, between the intellect and feeling. I have always felt more at ease with those who act naturally through feeling than with those who act with design through the intellect.

My colleagues and I would gather daily in the Land O'Cakes, commiserating with each other over the stories we had worked on but which had not been published, or congratulating those whose stories had won banner headlines. We had often worked long hours on a story and seen no results at the end. No story in the newspaper, no overtime pay. Yet, difficult though it may be to believe today, the lack of overtime pay was not what upset us. We took a pride in our work and we were disappointed when the substance of a story did not live up to expectations. That was what upset us.

There are always periods on a newspaper when every story you are detailed to pursue monotonously fails to live up to expectations, like a sequence of losers on a racecourse. During the course of my first six months on the paper, I had a particularly long sequence of failures and I became morbidly convinced I would be sacked.

I chased stories in Moss Side and Didsbury, in Oldham and Rochdale, in Cheetham and Hulme, in Chorlton cum Hardy and Salford, and out in the towns and villages of Derbyshire and Cheshire. Nothing went right for me. Every story I was sent to cover evaporated away as soon as I began to delve into it.

One evening in the Land O'Cakes I confided my despair to a colleague, John Redfern, a reporter of great experience, known by all of us as the bishop. He had already given me an insight into the ways of a first-class reporter by giving me a lesson on how to interview a potential informant; a lesson I have borne in mind ever since.

I accompanied him one day on a murder story and listened to him putting inane questions, or inane they seemed to me, to several people who lived in the neighbourhood of the murder. At last, innocently, I asked him why he had asked such inane questions. He grinned: 'To make them think I'm as stupid as you think I am.'

The point he had made, and which I have always remembered, is that you have a weapon in hand if you are underestimated.

I confided to him my despair over my run of failed

stories and he suggested a solution to my predicament. There we were, standing at the bar of the Land O'Cakes, each with a pint of beer, John wearing his owlish spectacles, his voice theatrically resonant like a bishop conducting a service:

'My dear fellow,' he said, mock pompously, 'all difficult problems have simple answers. What you have to do is to break this sequence of failure by acting out of character. Write a feature article! Get an idea, research on it, write it . . . and the sub-editors will be thankful to have something to fill up their early editions . . . and you'll have your name up, dear fellow.'

I decided to write an article about the Jubilee celebrations of the Kings and Queens of England, and I proceeded to spend spare day after spare day closeted in the Manchester Library . . . the very same building where I had now been invited to speak.

I collected large slices of historical interest from the books on the shelves and, in due course, my article appeared for two editions and I was naïvely thrilled because my name was in print at last. But it was not the article which secured my future and saved me from the sack. It was a funny incident of magical luck that saved me.

One late afternoon, after I had spent most of the day researching in the Library, I went for a long walk and, by chance, came to Chester Road, Hulme, and paused at the window of an antique shop. The owner saw me standing there and asked me in; he seemed to be in high excitement. I thought this strange because owners of antique shops are generally phlegmatic personalities, but I soon learnt the cause of his excitement. He had just acquired a 1639 edition of the Bible printed by Thomas Buck and Roger Daniel of Cambridge . . . but it was the place where the Bible had been found which ended my sequence of story failures. The Bible had been found floating in the Rochdale Canal.

Now here was I again in Manchester, Jeannie beside me, staying at the Midland Hotel, a late Victorian building of high ceilings and large rooms where Mr Rolls first met Mr Royce. It is an hotel which has been the scene of many dramas, mostly theatrical, and it was here that I suddenly found myself interviewing my theatrical gods like C. B. Cochran, André Charlot, Noël Coward, Gertrude Lawrence, and finding to my astonishment that they were trying to impress *me*, the reporter.

That evening, when we arrived at the Midland, I said to Jeannie we would dine in the French Restaurant, where Paul used to be restaurant manager. Paul was kind to me and allowed me credit, but there was one occasion when he was too kind, when he allowed me too much credit. I had invited two girls from a Charlot revue to after-theatre supper and Paul had led us to a table beside a pillar which stretched up to the high ceiling like a column in a cathedral. I had sat there with the two pretty girls, one on each side of me, lavishing hospitality that I could not afford. Over the years I had had this wish, this niggling wish, to see that pillar again.

'First,' I said to Jeannie, 'I want to go for a walk on my own.'

No tiresome objections on her part. Manchester, she realised, was my world. It did not belong to her.

Thus, I left the Midland and went out into the night, turned right after leaving the entrance, and walked up Moseley Street. I was on my way to the Land O'Cakes. I was on a sentimental journey. I wanted to stand at the bar of the Land O'Cakes and be aware again of the fun I once enjoyed there, and remember my companions like John Redfern, Brian Chapman, who was the editor, Mackenzie Porter, Geoffrey Murray, Guy Morgan, Roland Thornton, Jack Monk, Lobby Ludlow and Ronald Hyde. Ronald Hyde joined the *Daily Express* a month after me. He also was on trial. He was my rival and I watched him carefully, encouraged by his failures, apprehensive at his successes. But no need to worry. We both were kept on and we became best friends; and it so happens there is the engaging rook who now haunts Minack. We call it Ronald.

I crossed Market Street and into Oldham Street and,

when I reached the Oldham Street–Church Street junction, I had a sudden recall of the night I had a date with a slim, beautiful Cochran Young Lady, as the C. B. Cochran chorus girls were termed. I came off duty at eleven o'clock, jumped into my ancient Alvis car and rushed off with keen anticipation to keep my appointment with the girl at the Opera House stage door. I sped down Oldham Street at the same time as a taxi sped out of Church Street, and the taxi hit the Alvis broadside on. There was confusion, I was dazed, the Alvis just missed a lamp post, and the offside mudguard was crushed against the wheel. The accident could have been more serious, but it was serious enough for me. I missed my date with the slim, beautiful Cochran Young Lady.

I went on up Oldham Street and came to the pub called The Castle; the pub which was second home to the reporters of the *Daily Express* after the Land O'Cakes. Three pretty sisters used to live and work there, guarded over by a battle-axe of a mother. My particular sister was Nora, the youngest, and we used to sit on a step of the narrow staircase which curved to the rooms above, or Nora would fetch the key and open the door at the end of the dingy ground-floor passage, and we would go into what was known as the party room, where there was an upright mahogany-cased piano. Here I would play my version of *Rhapsody in Blue* and *I'll See You Again*, and Nora would lean against the piano and watch me.

Now, here I was, all these years later, entering The Castle again and, to my astonishment, nothing had changed. The same curved staircase, the same dingy ground-floor passage, the same door. Any moment Nora might have appeared, or her battle-axe of a mother, or two of my colleagues seeking Nora's sisters.

I had a drink, then on again up Oldham Street, and into Ancoats Street, and right to the Land O'Cakes with the glass *Express* building opposite.

'Whisky and soda, please,' I said to the man at the bar.

He gave me a gin and lime and was sullen when I pointed out the mistake.

I stood there, glass in hand, and gazed at the framed photostats of notable *Daily Express* stories on the walls; stories that went back to my time; headlines shouting as if it were news of today, enveloping me momentarily with the illusion that time had stood still and I was standing again with the fun of my colleagues around me.

Few were in the bar but, to one side, there were two men, unmistakable in appearance, unmistakable successors to my own colleagues, and I edged near them. One of them, florid-faced, was talking vehemently and I caught phrases like: 'He shouldn't have done it' . . . and . . . 'We must have a meeting.' I hovered a few feet away, hoping that a telepathic message would reach them that here was a man who also used to stand at the bar after crossing the road from the *Express* building, and who talked vehemently, unwinding after the day's work. But no telepathic message reached them and so, although aware it was the wrong thing to do, I hesitatingly broke in with a weak:

'Excuse me . . . I used to be on the *Express* myself.'

They looked at me wearily, and I, hoping to buy their attention, quickly asked the barman to refill their glasses.

'I'm making a pilgrimage,' I said, now falsely bright. 'This pub gave me lots of hangovers and lots of happy times.'

Their response, although polite, did not give me confidence, and I began to gush and say things of no significance; and they watched me, and I imagined they were thinking what on earth was I talking about. As I floundered, a corner of my mind was remembering that first time I'd entered the Land O'Cakes, the first time I had entered any pub, on my way with Guy Morgan to watch him at work at the Town Hall.

As I left to return to Jeannie to have our dinner together at the French Restaurant, I asked the florid gentleman if he would like to have drinks with me at noon next day and meet Jeannie. We waited, but he never came.

I returned to the Midland after my sentimental journey

and, while we were changing, I said: 'What moment in *your* life would you choose for a sentimental journey?'

'Pinchaford,' she replied.

'I guessed it would be Pinchaford.'

'Pinchaford opened my eyes and mind just as Manchester did for you. I think I was only thirteen when I went there first. Daddy saw the advertisement in *The Times*, a farm with horses on the edge of Dartmoor, and he sensed that it would be the sort of holiday I would like, and Barbara went with me, and it was just what Daddy thought it would be.'

Barbara is Jeannie's sister.

'There were four brothers,' Jeannie went on, 'and their mother, and they all took a share in running it as an easy-going farm guesthouse, and I liked one brother and another liked me. It was all such careless fun; up soon after dawn and going out to collect the horses in the field; riding over the moors, the smell of bracken and summer gorse, the freedom from all the petty formalities we had at home . . . there was John Smith who longed to be in journalism like me, and we had this in common, and he used to come to Pinchaford in August when we were there, and I remember John's mother who lost John's father in the First World War, and who cherished John the more for that. Pinchaford would be my sentimental journey. Two of the brothers were killed in the war. John was in the RAF and he was killed. It was extraordinary, but just one week after John was killed, a bomb in an air raid fell on Mrs Smith's house in Baron's Court. Almost as if she had wished it on herself.'

I was silent for a moment. I was thinking of those young men who died, and of their successors who are searching for values to believe in.

'You'll make your sentimental journey to Pinchaford one day,' I said, 'but now back to silliness. I am about to satisfy a niggling wish. Let's go.'

Niggling wishes, niggling feelings are not easily definable. They have no body in time, they are just irritations, like an itch. One can be niggled by the belief that one has made a remark one should not have made, or by the fear that a letter just posted is in an envelope addressed to somebody else, or that one cut an acquaintance by mistake in the street, or that one behaved foolishly at a party, or one has a persistent desire to do something, or to see someone and, by so doing, the desire will stop niggling. The essence of niggling feelings, niggling wishes, is that they are unimportant . . . as unimportant as seeing a pillar.

We entered the restaurant, high-ceilinged, well-spaced tables, greeted by the Paul of today, and he led us to a banquette at the side of the restaurant and, as I sat down, I was looking around for my pillar as if I were looking for an old friend.

'There it is!'

And the Paul of today looked startled.

'There it is!' I said to Jeannie.

Across the restaurant to my right was my pillar, smoothly rounded, pretending to be marble . . . 'There, Jeannie, is the cause of my niggling wish!'

A lifetime away I had sat beside that pillar, the two pretty girls from the Charlot revue calling for champagne and oysters, and more champagne and oysters. A boisterous, romantic, happy occasion. It took me six months of weekly instalments to pay the bill.

Now I was home, sitting in the corner of the sofa with Oliver on my lap, beginning our inquest.

'A pity,' said Jeannie, 'about Ackers Street. I'd have loved to have seen Number 10.'

'Number 56 Portsmouth Street was more important. It was there that I lived for over a year, looked after by a quiet little woman called Miss Robinson, the kindest landlady anyone could ever know.'

Both Ackers Street and Portsmouth Street are now smothered by the spreading buildings of Manchester University.

I paused.

Then: 'It didn't go *too* badly?' I said, questioningly, hopefully, the inevitable doubt of an amateur who has made a speech and goes on doubting long, long after the speech has been made.

'You know it was all right . . . one of the organisers said it was the most successful meeting there had been all the year.'

'I made a mistake reading those excerpts from the books . . .'

'That was my fault,' Jeannie said. 'It was my idea.'

'And there was the mistake I made by not speaking close enough to the mike. After two minutes, I saw a lot of blank faces in front of me, and that was when I asked— "can you hear me?"—and there was that answering chorus of "NO!" '

'You put it right.'

'Everybody was very, very nice . . . but I have to admit my confidence was dented.'

Those who introduce a speaker, or those who interview, can spur or destroy. So much depends on *rapport* between interviewer and interviewed, and whether the interviewer has done his homework. When Jeannie's novel *Home is the Hotel* was published, she was interviewed for a radio programme by a lady who had not even troubled to read the summary of the story on the book jacket. There was an occasion when I was sitting on the platform about to open a fête, when the elderly chairman, halfway through his introduction suddenly stopped, then bent down to me as I sat beside him and whispered desperately: 'What's your name?'

Oliver had begun to purr, and I traced a finger down his black, silky back.

'You don't have to have any regrets,' said Jeannie, encouragingly, 'I can assure you.'

I laughed.

'Why laugh?'

'I was thinking,' I said, 'of the time you opened the Mousehole Harbour Sports. It was a hot day and you rehearsed your speech all morning, standing naked on the rocks, speaking to a very still sea . . . and when you made the speech the mike went dead, and no one heard a word.'

'I had a very nice morning in the sun.'

Jeannie bent down and took a log from the basket and placed it on the fire. The gesture, for some reason, disturbed Oliver and he jumped off my lap.

'I wonder where Ambrose is?' said Jeannie.

'On a nocturnal hunt, I expect.'

'I'd like him to be here with us.'

'I'll go and look for him. Where's the torch?'

I got up and wandered around the room. It is odd how often when I want a torch I cannot find it.

'Here it is,' said Jeannie, picking it up from beneath the dresser; 'and, look, I've got this chunk of bread which is too hard for us. The donkeys will love it. They deserve an unexpected treat.'

I took the bread and went out into the night.

SIX

I basked in a sense of relief, like fulfilling a date to the dentist, now that the visit to Manchester was over. It had been enjoyable enough, but I no longer had to wake up in the night, doze for a second, then suddenly have a twist of anxiety when I realised that ahead of me, first months, then weeks, then days, was my speech and my facing an audience. Jeannie and I could now return to normality, prepare for Christmas, look forward to the daffodil season . . . and enjoy tenuous pleasures that have an affinity with magic. Nothing logical about such pleasures. No man-made gloss.

There was, for instance, Merlin's maiden voyage on the donkey walk. Margaret told us that one morning during our absence, she watched Merlin careering around the field and behaving as if he were longing for Fred to play with him, but Fred solidly ignored him. He raced round and round, flashing past Fred, flinging out his hind legs as he did so, and Margaret said that when at last he came to a stop, he looked disconsolate. He was disappointed by Fred's attitude. Fred was behaving like a superior elder brother. He did not approve of such frivolous antics.

I had sympathy for Merlin. It was a question of a donkey generation gap. Fred did not appreciate Merlin's zest for pleasure because he had forgotten his own zest at Merlin's age. He wanted quiet, orderliness, predictability. He did not want to be jerked out of his comfortable routine by a boisterous, experiment-questing juvenile. He accepted Merlin as a companion, but not as a coltish playmate.

Jeannie and I, on the other hand, had to be fair to Merlin. He was so full of the joy of living that we could not treat him simply as a companion to Fred. We had to cater for his zest, and so we decided it was time to take him on the donkey walk.

The donkey walk leads from Minack along the cliff to Carn Barges, then inland along a path with bramble tendrils stretching across it and gorse on either side which, at places, is so high that you seem to be walking through a tunnel without a top. Then on through a copse of may trees and blackthorn until you reach a stream. It is a stream which stopped Fred when he was young. Merlin, I suspected, would be stopped too.

We put on their halters and set off. It was a brisk, fine morning and across the Bay was the ribbon of the Lizard and so clear that we could easily see the white mushrooms of the Goonhilly Space Station. Jeannie held Fred and I held Merlin and, as soon as we began to walk down the cliff path, Merlin began to tug at the halter.

'He wants to go first,' I said.

'So I see,' said Jeannie, with sedate Fred.

Merlin and I swept past them. The rope of the halter was of nylon, and nylon is slippery to hold.

'Slow down, Merlin,' I said, and I jerked on the rope and nearly lost my hold on it.

'Steady, Merlin.'

We had now reached the low hedge with an earth top, the eastern boundary of Minack where, every year, I fix a typed notice on a board which says: HOPE YOU ENJOY YOUR WALK THROUGH THESE PRIVATE BULB MEADOWS ALONG THE PATH WHICH IS MARKED. PLEASE DO NOT FEED THE DONKEYS. It is a hedge which, over the years, has caused problems both to Fred, and to Penny his mother. Sometimes they jumped up and over without showing any inhibitions about doing so, and sometimes they treated it as if it were Beecher's Brook. Many a time

Fred has reached it, come to a full stop, shuffled his feet, approached it again, backed from it, while Jeannie and I have patiently waited for him to regain his nerve.

No inhibitions as far as Merlin was concerned. No need for patience on my part. He and I reached the hedge and I, apprehensive that when he arrived on the other side of the hedge he might hurtle away towards Carn Barges, took a firm hold of the slippery rope. This did not influence Merlin. He made me feel like a man tied to a runaway car. He leapt on to the top of the hedge as if unaware that I was holding him, and so I had to leap also, then flounder on the other side as Merlin, highly excited, attempted to race away into a new world of discovery.

'How funny you look,' laughed Jeannie.

I had momentarily fallen on the grass, still holding the slippery rope, half kneeling, Merlin's woolly face above me. At this moment, he calmed down. He calmed down enough to look at me with surprise, as if he were wondering what he could possibly have done to put me into such a position. Then Fred came up and nudged him and, by that time, I was on my feet and the four of us were on our way again.

Jeannie and I talk on the walk, not in the form of a conversation, but spasmodically. If I am leading, as I was with Merlin, Jeannie would be a few yards behind me and Fred, by now off his halter, in between. Fred was safe off the halter, as was Penny; but for the moment, I was taking no risks with Merlin. Merlin had to be educated in the routine of the donkey walk. There were certain rules to obey, certain temptations to avoid. I firmly held the slippery rope as he hurried along the path; not a straight path nor an even path, and there were boulders to hinder the way, which Merlin took in his stride, with me dutifully following.

'He's so confident,' I called back to Jeannie, 'that it seems he's been here before and knows where he's going.'

At that moment a cloud of starlings swept in from the sea, a whirling cloud like a swarm of bees, and Merlin was momentarily forgotten.

'The Scandinavians have arrived!' came from Jeannie.

She always called the starlings, which arrived in winter, Scandinavians. She may be right in doing so. I do not know. Certainly I believe that the clouds of starlings which come to Britain in the winter produce one of the most strange phenomena I have ever seen. How, as they whirl in the sky in their thousands, do they not collide? Has anyone seen a collision? Has anyone seen a starling catastrophe in the manner of two aircraft colliding in the sky? Not a tiny piece of explanation has ever been produced as to how their fantastic manoeuvres take place without accidents. Only magic is the answer. 'Further investigation,' wrote Gilbert White, 'mocks man's prying pride.'

I do not suppose I would approve of them if Minack wood were one of their roosting centres at night; one of those centres where thousands gather, chatter, sleep, chatter, then split up into parties in the morning to sweep round the countryside, descending upon pastures like black confetti from the sky. I would object to the noise and the muck, but I would be impotent if I tried to turn them away. Roosting centres have been used from time immemorial, just as from time immemorial the role of the starling has been vital for the countryside. Its activities have been nature's way of cleansing the ground and, despite the spread of chemicals, they continue to do so. Leather-jackets, beetles and their larvae, wireworm, woodlice, slugs, pests of all kinds are the victims.

We reached Carn Barges and turned inland and, by that time, my confidence in Merlin's behaviour was growing.

'Jeannie,' I said, 'I think I can take off his halter.'

'You had better be careful.'

'I'll walk ahead of him and with you behind Fred they will be in a sandwich between us and there can't be any risk.'

As it was, there was no risk on the outward journey, and I was correct in my expectation that, when we reached the stream, Merlin would behave as Fred had done at Merlin's age. Fred, on this occasion, jumped the stream in the manner of an old hand at the game, but Merlin, Merlin had one look at the three-feet-wide running water, and backed away, side-stepped into the winter-beaten bracken and undergrowth. He, as Fred had been, was scared.

This amused Fred. He had scored a point against Merlin. Merlin might be receiving special attention because he was new to the scene but he, Fred, was in command. He had demonstrated it. He had no fear of jumping the stream, but this boisterous Merlin was scared.

Merlin, however, on our way back, had recovered his nerve and his boisterousness. I led the way, Merlin still off the halter, and we passed again through the tunnel of gorse, then down the foot-wide path with the bramble tendrils stretching across and, those that I failed to cut with my secateurs on the outward journey, I now cut as I returned and, as I paused to do so, Merlin nudged me with his nose in my back. A December morning, very quiet, salt scents from the sea, a raven croaking, flying west towards Land's End, a stonechat bobbing its tail as it watched us from a boulder, and all of us enjoying ourselves.

'I was thinking,' I said, after Merlin had given me another nudge in the back to tell me to walk faster, 'that most of the basics which make up happiness are corny.'

I had spoken, looking ahead, and Jeannie behind me, behind two donkeys as well, only heard a mumble.

'Speak up. I couldn't hear.'

'Most of the basics of happiness are corny.'

'And what does that mean?'

'Telling other people how to live their lives is an industry . . . politicians, the media, academics, intellectuals, the churches, they are all part of the industry. And to keep the industry prosperous, they drench the public with their theories, confusing the public, leading them away from the obvious.'

The donkeys had stopped. A clump of out-of-season campion was being devoured.

'Go on.'

'The theories have to be complicated ones to keep the industry on the move; always promising results in the future, material or spiritual . . . and the obvious is ignored.'

'Which is?'

'The obvious revolves around the corny qualities of love and kindness.'

We were moving again and nearing Carn Barges, where we turn right and start on the final homeward stretch.

'You see, that's what I mean. Happiness is based on corny virtues. That is its weakness. It is too simple for this complicated world . . . and it provokes giggles. Some people are always ready to giggle at simplicity.'

I heard the laugh of Jeannie behind me.

'As simple and corny,' she said, 'as taking two donkeys a walk along a cliff!'

Suddenly I was knocked sideways, and I put out my hand to stop myself from falling, and it clasped a gorse bush.

'Merlin! Blast you!'

He had blazed past me, and I cursed myself for talking so much that I had forgotten to put on his halter for the last part of the walk.

He was away!

Then, a moment later, I was buffeted again. Fred rushed by in pursuit.

I had had many previous experiences of such a situation. Penny would suddenly make a dash to freedom, followed by Fred, and always my reaction would be the same. It was the same on this occasion. As Fred dashed past, I grabbed at his tail, caught it, tried to hold on, was treated like an incompetent tug-of-war team . . . and then let go.

I watched them both snake at speed along the path and I said to Jeannie that their escape was not all that important because they would only end up over the stone hedge in Minack fields and then could go no further. They might cause a problem when we tried to catch them, mocking us as we approached them with the halters, running away just as we reached them, but they could come to no harm. They could never go further than the Pentewan boundary.

I had, however, as they snaked at speed along the path, forgotten a badger track that led at right angles from the path up a steep bank and into a disused field, which itself was part of the moorland we looked upon from the cottage windows. From the disused field, a track led through the moorland, past the shadows of hedges guarding long-ago meadows, up a gently sloping hill, then on through other moorland until it turned down the hill and joined our lane, And then, of course, the lane led to the farm and farm buildings of Jack Cockram, Walter Grose and Bill Trevorrow, and wound its way on to the main road.

Suddenly I saw Merlin turn right and up the steep bank, climbing it like a goat. Then Fred, shedding his sedate, elder brother role, made a dash after him, and they both disappeared from view.

'Now we're in trouble,' I said.

'You should have put on his halter,' said Jeannie.

I was cross with myself, and I was cross with Jeannie for rubbing in the obvious.

'What shall we do?'

'Only one thing possible,' I said. 'We have to follow them and pray they've found a patch of grass where they are grazing.'

A minute later, we had clambered up the steep bank and into the disused field, and there were no donkeys in sight.

'Now we're in real trouble,' I said. 'They've taken to the track and, at the speed they were going, they could be on the lane and up past the farm buildings by now.'

'They could have stopped on the way.'

'We'll soon find out.'

We set off, hurrying up the track, wind-flat bracken on either side of us, and the yellow sparkle of winter-flowering gorse, and the brambles dangling along the track waiting to trip us.

76

'Perhaps,' said Jeannie, 'they've stopped by the badger sett. Fred used to stop there with Penny.'

We look out across the shallow valley upon this badger sett from the cottage. It is a vast sett and has been in existence, who knows, for aeons of time; long before man aspired to a sophisticated civilisation. Twice, during our years at Minack, it has been gassed. I remember the first time this happened, Jeannie and I hurried in the Land Rover we had then to see Jack Edwards, a retired game-keeper, who kept a pub at Connor Downs near Hayle, and Jeannie told him of her distress that the badgers had been murdered in such a way. It was April, and the cubs had died too.

'Sad enough now,' said Jack, 'but be sure the badgers will be back. They always come back. Setts like that have been badger homes for a thousand years and more . . . they won't be defeated by man.'

Jack Edwards was right. Within a couple of years the sett was in use again, entrances were re-opened, tracks to them were trodden down and, on early summer evenings, I would sometimes watch from the cottage with my field-glasses and see the cubs emerging as dusk fell; and when in luck I would, for a few minutes, watch them play.

A while after their return to the sett, another witch-hunt against badgers began. On controversial evidence, they had been accused of bringing tuberculosis to cattle; evidence which was difficult to believe to be accurate. Badgers are the cleanest animals imaginable. The hygiene in their setts, hygiene being a word well-favoured by humans, is accepted by every badger student as impeccable. They are, in fact, the only European wild animal which regularly removes its own bedding and replaces it with fresh.

However, the witch-hunt was set in motion, sponsored by the Ministry of Agriculture, and sometimes setts were gassed and sometimes the badgers were caught by a particularly cruel kind of trap. Thereupon a form of guerrilla war was conducted by those who wanted to protect the badgers, and I know of one farmer who refused, despite being threatened that he would be taken to Court, to allow the Ministry men on his land; and when they proceeded to set traps on his neighbour's land, he sneaked over the hedge at night and set them off. At St Just near Cape Cornwall, the vicar conducted his own campaign to stop the gassing of a sett in the vicarage garden where his children had a tree-house above the sett. Apart from wishing to protect the badgers, whose activities had become part of the children's lives, he was concerned about the cyanide which was used, the possible effect on water supplies, the risk of its use to children and to local pets, and the way the tins which contained the cyanide powder were buried in the setts. The Ministry men had soothing answers to all these fears, quoting a Ministry leaflet which stated that 'occupiers are advised to keep children and pets away from blocked setts for at least a fortnight after gassing has been completed'. But what might happen during that fortnight? As for traps, Jeannie and I once rescued a victim of one. It was a dog, a beagle. We rescued it in the early hours of one morning. The trap was attached to a low branch of a tree and in such a manner that the dog's paw was hoisted off the ground, tight in a thick wire. It took me five minutes to cut through it.

We were now nearing the sett and the plateau of scrubland where Penny and Fred used to pause. Away to our left was the cottage, snug in the side of the low hill, and stretching inland away from it were the bare trees of Minack wood. Just a few yards up a steep slope, and we would be in sight of the plateau; in sight too, we prayed, of two donkeys.

'They are there!'

Jeannie was in front of me.

'Thank goodness!'

'How are we going to catch them?'

There were two exits from the plateau of scrubland. One exit was the track up which we had walked, the other exit was the track which led eventually to our lane and up to the farm buildings. We had to manoeuvre the donkeys so that both exits were blocked. This was a tricky task. One glance at Merlin and I saw that, colloquially speaking, he was relishing the taste of the honey. This unsupervised freedom was so enjoyable that he wanted more of it. Thus, when I advanced towards him, halter in hand, he allowed me to get within a few feet, and then he darted away.

'Jeannie,' I said, 'if I stay by the lane exit and you try to shepherd Fred towards me, we might at least be able to catch *him*.'

I should have been annoyed, but I wasn't. This was a game, an unimportant, trivial game of trying to corral two donkeys. It was fun.

'Go on, Fred . . . go on. Go on!'

Jeannie was flapping the halter; Fred was moving away from her, but not in my direction. He had observed the position where I stood, knew what we were up to, and had no intention of surrendering his unsupervised freedom without an effort. He was aiming to outflank Jeannie, then dash down the track whence we had come.

'Fred,' I shouted, 'it's your job to set a good example. This is Merlin's first donkey walk and it's proving a disaster. Pull yourself together! Behave yourself!'

If you speak to a donkey in this manner, you may hope for co-operation, but you will not get it.

'Fred!'

He bucked. He flung out his hind legs, then spurted away, fortunately not towards the cliff exit, but to a far corner. A second later, he was joined by a joyful, prancing Merlin. Two donkeys in rebellion against conventionality.

'Now what are we going to do?'

'We'll appeal to Fred's greed,' said Jeannie.

'And his curiosity,' I said.

'Yes.'

It was a device we had used many times before when Fred had refused to obey. It was a simple trick which he could not resist. All we had to do was to tear up some grass, roll it into a ball, hold it in a hand, and offer it to him as if it were a carrot or some other donkey delight.

'Here, Fred, look what I've got.'

Jeannie was speaking. She spoke gently, coaxingly.

'Come on, Fred.'

He was several yards away, munching.

'Fred . . . you'll like this.'

A wicked deception, but necessary.

'Fred . . . !'

He was not responding. Perhaps we had played the trick too often. He was wise to it. He went on munching as if he were saying to himself . . . 'Let her go on holding out her hand until she is tired of it.'

A buzzard floated high overhead, mewing, and then I heard the answering cry of another. No other sound except the rumble of the sea.

'He's making fools of us,' I said. Jeannie standing in desolate scrubland with her hand held out; me with a halter beside her.

'Fred may be doing so,' Jeannie said, 'but see what's happening over there.'

Over there was Merlin. He had no experience of our trick. He thought we were genuine. When he espied Jeannie holding out her hand enticingly, he obviously conjured up in his memory other hands held out enticingly, other hands offering donkey delights. And his woolly legs, resembling old-fashioned plus-fours, were hastening as quickly as they could towards us.

Merlin slid to a stop, ears pricked, pushing his nozzle towards Jeannie's outstretched hand. Youth about to be deceived.

'Quick, put on the halter.'

I had noticed, soon after his arrival, that Merlin had the habit of pushing his nozzle forward when I was about to put on his halter, as if he had been trained to expect this way of fixing it. Thus he expected the bottom loop of the halter to go first over his nozzle, then followed by the second loop over his ears . . . always with Fred I had done it the other way round. I was now to be grateful for his training. He proceeded to push his nozzle forward in

expectation of receiving the delight in Jeannie's outstretched hand . . . and received, instead, the loop of the
halter.

'Caught!' I said, triumphantly.

'I'll give you a biscuit later, Merlin,' said Jeannie,
apologetically.

He surrendered gracefully.

And that was the end of Merlin's first donkey walk.

SEVEN

A crisp, January morning; frost up country, but none at Minack since winter began. The wind is our enemy, our perpetual enemy. Frost makes darting attacks, ice on the water butt that has melted by noon. Frost is not a perpetual enemy like the wind; nor is snow. Frost and snow flirt with us; but when, year after year, we are lulled into thinking that the flirtation is harmless, they will suddenly cause us dismay. The pipe from the well is frozen, no bath water, no drinking water, and I have to take a pail to Monty's Leap and scoop from the stream. Twice, only twice have we been snowed up . . . the lane, drift deep, a white river between us and the farm at the top of the hill.

No prospect of snow on this crisp, January morning; no prospect of frost. It is one of those clean Cornish winter days, when the horizon is clear and the sea sparkles in the sun and the gulls float above the cliffs, and early wallflowers scent their yellow petals. Down by Monty's Leap are the sprawling Ascania violets, and Charlie the chaffinch sits on a fuchsia branch close to the bird table, calling for his favourite sunflower seeds. And up on the roof, a respectful distance between each other, Ronald the rook and Philip the gull wait to scramble for whatever it is that Jeannie chooses to throw to them.

A crisp, January morning and the time for a stroll up the winding lane with Oliver and Ambrose and, as we strolled, we were aware of one special advantage of the life we were leading. No stress to be endured travelling to work, travelling back home. No pummelling in tube trains, no queuing for buses, no traffic jams, no din. We had experienced these discomforts and now we were free, but it was a freedom which could never be taken for granted. Hence when we strolled up the lane with Oliver and Ambrose, we thought of those in the trains, buses and traffic jams and had what may seem to be a strange wish: that each of those who hated their daily travel could miraculously, always on their own, transport themselves to the winding lane.

Not that Oliver or Ambrose would enjoy their arrival. They scurry from strangers. True, as Oliver grew older, he would allow me to pick him up and not struggle as I talked to a stranger. He blinked at them, toleration blinks, not a sign of enjoying their praise of him. Oliver was above the flattery of human praise, like a believer in that simple philosophical truism that flattery has little value when you know your own worth. Oliver knew he was a very remarkable cat. Thus only good manners let him tolerate strangers. But Ambrose . . . Ambrose continued as he had always been, wanting to be on his own, hating strangers, a ginger flash racing away as soon as a stranger appeared.

Just past the gate, on the way up the lane, on the right a few yards into the undergrowth was the house I built for Oliver when he was courting us, when Lama was keeping him at bay. It was a very little house. I collected hedge stones and placed them as walls and, for a roof, I used a polythene fertiliser bag resting on wooden battens and this I covered with bracken. Ivy creeps over the little house now, strands falling over the entrance but, as we passed it on that crisp, January morning, Oliver sauntered to inspect it. Nothing unusual. He often did so. It was as if he had fond memories of it, not because of its comforts, but because it was the first indication that I might be prepared to make him welcome.

He was very shy at the time. He would hover in the lane, run away when Jeannie approached with a saucer, only reappearing after she had put it down and left. He courted us for two years, including two Christmases, before Lama died, and he was accepted in the cottage.

On that first Christmas night, we were entertaining Beverley Nichols, worshipper of cats. He was intrigued far more in how Oliver was enjoying his Christmas evening alone in his little house in the undergrowth than in the dinner Jeannie had provided. As soon as dinner was over, therefore, Beverley urged Jeannie, who needed little urging, to chop up some breast of turkey on to a saucer and he carried it down to Oliver in his house, while Jeannie carried a saucer of milk. It was a windy night, cold and, earlier in the evening, there had been a flurry of snow, and the trees talked in the wind as the three of us, torch in my hand pointing the way, walked down the lane and across Monty's Leap on the happy mission of giving Oliver a Christmas feast.

Jeannie placed the saucer a few feet away from the little house and proceeded to make those curious noises which human beings are apt to make when trying to inveigle the attention of a cat. Beverley too made noises. They were, in fact, very sophisticated cat-inveigling noises, and for good reason. He had spent a long lifetime inveigling cats, winning them, loving them, becoming their slave and, while doing so, he had also been a student of the ways people behaved towards cats. Thus he came to the eventual conclusion that the human race was divided into two classifications: F and non-F. The letter F being short for Feline.

The F game is a good one to play; a subtle one. Look around those you know and see how you would label them. Clearly, in Beverley's assessment, F people are more sensitive than non-F. Non-F people are inclined to be worthy, logical, extrovert and to lack imagination. That definition may sound a little harsh, but it gives an idea of what is meant by non-F. F people are more complicated . . . dreamers, impractical planners, romantic, possessing extra-sensory powers and unashamed of being sometimes sentimental. Nor is that definition foolproof. I have met very practical people who are F; though, now I come to think of it, I have never met a dreamer who is non-F. Except myself. I was brought up in a non-F environment and only became F when I married Jeannie. Or perhaps it would be fairer to say that it was only then that I became aware that I had, in fact, been a secret F all along.

The inveigling noises continued while the wind blew through the trees. No sight of Oliver except for a second when he peered round the entrance of his house and the light of my torch reflected in two fluorescent yellow eyes. Cats the world over would have been thrilled to receive such attention, would have responded gladly to such coaxing, and the ambitious among them would have realised that here could be the chance to achieve stardom . . . a place in the Beverley Nichols annual Cat Calendar.

But not Oliver.

Oliver, even faced by turkey temptation, was not going to be lured out of his house. He had dignity and style. He was not going to stoop into obeying any inveigling requests for him to appear, for him to gobble his turkey in public.

And so there was a whispered consultation and the inveigling noises were stopped and the three of us departed from the lane, went through the gap into the greenhouse field, then delicately stepped to a point of the stone hedge where we could see where we had previously stood, where on the ground was the saucer with the chopped breast of turkey . . . and we waited. Silence. The great cat worshipper in overcoat with collar up, Jeannie wishing she was wearing something warmer, and myself, more detached than the other two, deciding that I would not shine the torch on Oliver if his shadow appeared. He wanted to enjoy his breast of turkey in privacy, and he would do so. Nor did Beverley and Jeannie want me to shine the torch on him. They accepted defeat and accepted their defeat with goodwill. Their inveigling noises had failed. Oliver was not going to invite them to the party. Their consolation was to put their hands on the hedge, take care not to be spiked by a branch of a blackthorn . . . and lean over the hedge, and eventually see a black outline appear from the undergrowth, and gobble.

Oliver was with Ambrose the following Christmas. How uncanny it was to have the double of Monty. No genetic explanation. No search for a double on our part. Just a magical moment when, standing by Monty's Leap, I saw this little ginger kitten appear from the undergrowth . . . and then saw Oliver rush up to him and lick him. The ginger double of Monty and the black double of Lama, and there they were that second Christmas of Oliver's, outside the porch, the lights of the Christmas tree shining on them . . . hoping to come in . . . while Jeannie and I were tending to the dying days of Lama.

But here they were, strolling up the lane with us, each pausing from time to time to stare at the bordering grass, hoping for an unexpected diversion. And when nothing materialised, one would go to the other, nudging, and Jeannie would say as they did so: 'Look at those two, bumping and boring.'

Animals for me represent a form of anchor in my life; a reassurance, a symbol that in this world of envy, greed and humbug, innocence exists. Such a sentimental summary may not meet with approval. This functional age despises sentiment. It always surprises me that violence is accepted as a way of life, but not sentiment. A hint of sentiment, and it will be met with smirks. Violence, on the other hand, in plays, films, literature, whether in the role of mental or physical cruelty, is lauded. I suppose this is because violence is easier to mirror than sentiment. It is easier to shock than to soothe.

We had reached the turn in the lane, a hundred yards from Monty's Leap, when there was a hooting from Fred. He was in the stable meadow and he had seen our heads moving along above the hedge that bordered the lane, and he was obviously annoyed that we had not taken him with us. No hoot from Merlin. Indeed there had not been a hoot from Merlin since he arrived. Strange. Surely an eighteen-months-old donkey should by now have a voice?

On Christmas Eve we had introduced him to the mince-pie tradition. I do not remember when the tradition began, but it was soon after Penny and Fred came to Minack. It was Jeannie who suggested it, after she had listened to the tales of an old man who frequented a pub called the Engine at Cripplease on the hilly road between Penzance and St Ives. Although we had been long used to local old men telling us stories that were fanciful, we listened to him because he sounded so convincing . . . that he had often seen donkeys kneel down on the stroke of twelve on Christmas Eve. He even went further. He said that on one Christmas Eve he tied his donkey to a hook in its stable in such a way that he could not possibly kneel; and when a few minutes after midnight he went to have a look, the rope had been snapped and the donkey *was* kneeling.

Neither Jeannie nor myself truly believed his stories, but the following Christmas Eve she proposed that we might test the truth of them with Penny and Fred. As it happened, when the time came, when the minutes ticked closer to midnight, our nerve failed. It was better, we decided, to *imagine* the donkeys kneeling at midnight, not to prove it. Thus, at a few minutes to midnight, we left Penny and Fred on their own . . . after they had consumed, much to their greedy delight, a plateful of mince pies specially made for the occasion by Jeannie. Thus the Christmas Eve tradition of donkey mince pies began.

We had debated whether to cancel the tradition now that Penny had died. That last time, that last Christmas Eve, she had seemed quite normal as she followed us into the stables, Jeannie holding the plate of mince pies above her head, tantalisingly out of reach. I went to light the candle, the same candle lit every year, but when this time I struck a match, then another, and another, the candle failed to respond, and when at last the wick caught alight, the whole candle flared up like a firework, then melted into a gluey mess. As it did so, I remembered an old adage that a flaring candle bodes no good, and a shiver passed through me. A few days later, Penny died.

Our debate ended in a compromise. We decided to keep to the tradition but, for this Christmas Eve, we would change the timing and, instead of waiting until a quarter to midnight, we would have the party earlier in the evening. Thus Mingoose Merlin would have his introduction to the tradition, but we ourselves would escape the hurt of thinking: 'This time last year . . .' It was to prove an unfortunate compromise.

The mince pies were baked; we had supper, and around nine o'clock we went out into the night.

'Fred! Merlin!'

We had undone the rope that fastened the gate into the small yard in front of the stables, and out of this small yard was a narrow gap between the stable wall and the yard wall. Through this gap, in a few minutes, the donkeys answered our call. First Fred; then Merlin.

I was momentarily aware of feeling self-conscious. The keeping up of a tradition can make one feel self-conscious. What is the point of it? Why, once again, go through all the paraphernalia? Why, for that matter, have the ceremony of the opening of Parliament, or of Trooping the Colour, or any of the traditional ceremonies in towns and villages throughout the country? There is no rational answer. Some of the ceremonies may be of tourist value, but they all have one tenuous feature in common. Everyone, in the end, hungers for a past.

Jeannie and I went into the stables, Jeannie holding the plate of mince pies while I, instead of lighting a candle, placed my torch on a ledge so that it shone against the end wall, a rough, emulsion white wall, and the muted reflection gave the same effect as a candle, an effect of soft shadows and mystery and timelessness. We stood there, waiting for the donkeys, but they did not come.

'Come on, you two,' I said.

We could see Merlin facing us just outside the doorway.

'Merlin . . . this is an occasion. This is your first Christmas-Eve party.'

He remained motionless, a shaggy outline.

'Dangle a mince pie in front of him,' I suggested.

And Jeannie took a mince pie, and dangled it.

'Look what I've got for you, Merlin,' said Jeannie.

He took the bait, pushed his nose towards her and followed her as she retreated back into the stable.

'I'm not giving it to you yet,' she said, holding the mince pie away from him; 'not until Fred is here.'

But where was Fred?

'Fred!' I called. 'Fred! The party is about to begin!'

No sign.

I left Jeannie with Merlin and went outside into the darkness of the small yard, but Fred was no longer there. He had returned to the field and so I went through the gap after him, calling him, half wondering whether the reason for his obstinacy was his memory of other years. I found him standing a few yards away, bottom towards me and, as I had no halter with me, I could only try and push him back towards the stables. He had no wish to move. He stood solidly, anchored to the ground while I tried to turn him and, when at last I succeeded in doing this and began pushing, it was like trying to push a car up a hill. Gradually I edged him towards the gap, then through it and into the yard, and it seemed that the party could now begin.

Not so.

Nothing would induce Fred to enter the stables; not even the mince pies, which always in the past he had relished.

As for Merlin, he seized the mince pie Jeannie at last offered him, chewed it for a second . . . then spat it out.

Collecting the torch, we left the two of them there in the darkness and returned to the cottage. Jeannie and I were in the mood of a host and hostess whose party had been a disaster.

But there were other matters to think about as we strolled with Oliver and Ambrose on the return down the lane on that crisp, January morning. There were practical matters, for instance, such as how we were going to manage our twenty acres during the coming year. True, many of these acres represented cliff-land and croft, but there was more than enough working land to justify employing a regular help and, until recently, we had always employed such a help, Geoffrey. Geoffrey drove the tractor, rotovated the greenhouses, sterilised them, cared for the tomatoes, dug the bulbs, planted them, cleared the bulb meadows of bracken in the autumn, replaced the glass of the greenhouses if they were broken in storms, did the maintenance, while Jeannie and I played our parts as very necessary casual workers. But now we could not afford a regular help because the statutory wage had leapt, while in the same period the prices we'd received for tomatoes and daffodils had gone *down*. Thus, whatever we planned to do in the future had to be planned on the basis that there was only one person to do the heavy work. Me.

The compensations for being on our own, however, were many. The chains fell off us. We had become so consumed by the stress of trying to find ways to grow crops that would pay the wages, and then failing to do so, that we were losing our personal freedom. There we were, living in the setting of our dreams, and yet in chains. Such a situation is apt to breed side effects and we found ourselves groaning in the morning when we heard the sound of Geoffrey's motorbike ('What shall we get him to do today?'), and rejoicing when it was a weekend and we had the place to ourselves. Nerves are on edge, however amiable the employee, if the business is struggling to pay the weekly wage. There was another compensation. We could not now become onlookers, skimming along the surface of the life we had chosen, instead of living it. We were back to our earthy beginning . . . with a difference.

The difference, of course, concerned our comforts. Rain dripped through the roof on our first night at Minack and we had a water filter to catch the tadpoles that came from the water I drew from Monty's Leap. No bath. No electricity. Jeannie cooking on a paraffin stove which once burst into flames as she was frying eggs for breakfast.

The cottage was a derelict shell. No lane to reach it. The land around a jungle. We rented it. We still rent it, but every comfort that has come, every improvement that has been made, has been done by ourselves. We cherish Minack because, in spirit, we feel we own it, will always own it, long after we have gone.

Thus, in facing an earthy future, there was this difference. We now lived in the equivalent of a comfortable town flat. Electricity, with storage heaters; two freezers; television (but adamantly no telephone); running water from a thirty-feet-deep well (doubtful supply in summer). Calor gas in a kitchen resembling a ship's galley, designed by Jeannie; a spare bedroom which we bought as a chicken house; our own bedroom which is so small that there is difficulty in walking round the end of the bed, and a sun porch which we built, where we often eat, and which has a certain disadvantage. Philip the gull likes to strut on it, banging the glass with his beak as he does so.

Then there were the horticultural comforts, the machines which have made working the land progressively easier over the years and, in acquiring them, I always had the thought at the back of my mind that they were an insurance against the day I might be left to do the heavy work on my own. Some of them in the past have been failures. Some of them have been so mechanically unreliable that I have wondered whether they have been sabotaged by Cornish pixies who, no doubt, hate progress. I have spent many hours watching a mechanic tinker with an engine, a mechanic who would inevitably repeat the words of some previous mechanic: 'I don't know what can be wrong. I've never known this happen before.'

I had at my disposal, to aid me with the heavy work, the Japanese-made Brush Cutter which enabled me to surge through the autumn bracken in the multitude of small bulb meadows that terraced the cliffs; a Howard hand-controlled rotovator; a Condor motor scythe; a Leyland tractor; an electric hedge-cutter, operated from a battery and attached by a long flex; a small motorised saw; an electric hand drill; and a tiny motor hoe which I could steer between five inch rows. I viewed them all with suspicion. They were at my disposal, but they also could be dangerous. 'Be careful of the last half hour,' a farmer friend cheerfully warned me. 'That's when the accidents happen.'

On that crisp, January morning, Oliver and Ambrose bumping and boring, we discussed the programme for the coming months and came to a decision. After the daffodil season which would soon begin, after sowing the sweet peas, the green peas and the runner beans in the Orlyt greenhouse, after sowing the flower seeds, after planting the potatoes, after pulling up this year's sprouts and preparing the ground for next year's, after planting the Maascross tomatoes in the greenhouses C and D, after digging the ditch in the lane, after . . . we would take it easy. The secret of the self-employed, if there is the self-discipline to achieve it, is simply not to take on too much.

The snag is, however, that when one is self-employed, it is not just the hours one puts into the work that is at stake. There are the capital sums involved. And there are many people who, at a bold moment of their lives, have decided to throw away the security of a dull, remunerative job, for the wide open spaces of independence, and have invested in some project which, after the first great enthusiasm, begins to be a tyrant. It is like being black-mailed. The more you pay, the more is demanded of you. Jeannie and I have had this experience at Minack and as a consequence we were on guard. We were not going to allow ourselves to be under strain. We would not fall into the trap of being over-conscientious.

A few days later, it was a Friday, Jeannie always goes into Penzance on a Friday, she came back with the news that she had met the pedlar, who had just come back from the Scillies, and he'd told her that the flower season there was late. The pedlar had been an institution in West Cornwall and the Scillies for half a century, and he was now in his eighties. He had been known to generations of children as Uncle Albert and to many people as Cloggy, after the clogs he used to wear. His surname was Mellor, and although Jeannie and I had known him for many years we still did not call him Cloggy. He was Mr Mellor to us. The use of his surname seemed more to match his natural dignity. Thus if I were to see him on the road carrying his box of wares, bewhiskered, wearing a knitted wool beret with a pompom on top, I would draw up beside him and call: 'Can I give you a lift, Mr Mellor?'

It was as Mr Mellor that we once invited him to a Fred birthday party, where the schoolchildren of St Buryan milled round Fred and Penny, while he played his barrel-organ. His barrel-organ (he had two, one of them over a hundred years old), was as much a part of his fame as the box containing his wares. He bought them many years ago from an Italian immigrant in Manchester and, since then, Mr Mellor had played them countless times for charity, earning for charities many thousands of pounds. Collectors asked to buy them. They pressurised him, offering sums that you would not think he could refuse. 'Money's no value to me,' was his reply.

Mr Mellor was an anachronism. Money really had no value to him. He had the philosophy, the corny philosophy, of trusting people, of being kind, of being cheerful, of not being envious, of possessing the genuine wish to help without any thirst for recognition. This attitude was the currency by which he lived a happy life. I suppose he was as far as possible as free as the wind he faced every early morning as he walked the lanes of Cornwall . . . 'Can I give you a lift, Mr Mellor?'

Jeannie met him near the harbour, close by where he lives. A useful meeting, because at that time of the year it is valuable to know both the condition and timing of the daffodil crop in the Scillies. He had also, as always on his visits, seen Jane of *A Drake at the Door*, who lives and works on Tresco, the sub-tropical island of the Scillies. 'Took the two children a little present,' he said. Sylvia, the elder child, is our god-daughter. As for Jane, she is so knowledgeable about the plants of Tresco and the daffodil bulbs of the islands that, at the time of Mr Mellor's visit, she had just been invited to speak on them at the prestigious Cannington Agricultural College in Somerset. The same Jane, who at the age of fourteen had arrived barefoot at Minack, refusing to go back to school, saying she wanted to work with flowers.

The Scillies were late . . . but Mr Mellor had also said that the Soleil d'Or crop, the bread-and-butter crop of the Scillies, had been a good one and they had been sending to market since November. This news we could welcome. It so happens that the Soleil d'Or crop sometimes coincides with the beginning of the daffodil crop so, if the Soleil d'Or crop were out of the way, this would be a help to our own prospective market prices. On the other hand, if their daffodils were late, as Mr Mellor had said, and our daffodils were early, the two would clash. Every daffodil season Jeannie and I have the same tactical discussions, each discussion as fresh as if there had never been daffodil problems before.

However, there was this year one aspect of daffodil marketing about which we had to come to a firm decision, and this concerned the bud condition of the daffodils when we packed them for market. We had been dithering with the decision for the past two years, and the dithering had caused a mild conflict between Jeannie and myself. Jeannie had a purist's view about the condition of a daffodil which was sent to market, while I was commercially-minded. Jeannie wanted to send daffodils with the buds half-open, so the customer, when they reached the shop, could see the yellow petals. I, on the other hand, hardened by salesman advice, wanted to send them in tight bud.

This mild conflict mirrored other such conflicts between Jeannie and myself. Jeannie, for instance, was romantic in her attitude to flowers in the garden, while I, although agreeing with her in sentiment, was more practical. I look at a young wallflower or stock plant and wish to pinch out the centre so that the laterals will bush out. Jeannie prefers to leave the centre intact. I am in favour of the hard pruning of roses, Jeannie is hesitant about it. Jeannie, one year, stuck a number of geranium cuttings into the soil of the Orlyt and they blossomed, and they blossomed, so she left them there instead of adopting her original plan to transplant them into the garden.

Thus when, towards the end of January, the daffodil season was about to begin, I realised I would have to be both gentle and subtle if my views, my commercial views, were to succeed.

'Look,' I said, holding up a tight Magnificence bud I had just picked from a meadow down the cliff, 'this is the way the market wants to have them.'

'It's stupid! Who would want to buy a bunch of daffs looking like grass?'

The bud I held was as straight as a pencil, stem and bud seemed to be as one. No sign of the head dropping, not a suspicion of colour. The customer would not have a clue as to what kind of daffodil he was buying.

'Stupid, I agree . . . but that is how the market wants it. Now, I've got an idea . . . let's put it in a jar and see how long it takes to come out, if it does ever come out.'

Within a few years, market requirements had gone from one extreme to another. Not so long ago, the daffodils were forced into full bloom and a bud in a bunch was forbidden. Then began the period when growers (and we were very much in favour) were urged to send them in bud, but with a touch of yellow showing; and now there was this new revolution of marketing them looking like grass. I knew we would have to do it. Often, during the last season, the words scrawled across our invoice returns were: 'Too far open.'

Jeannie had to be persuaded. Jeannie had to move with the times. Jeannie, though very modern in her outlook, was slow to favour new methods, new gadgets. She was sceptical, had to be convinced of their value and, so slow was she, that our old friend the late A. P. Herbert liked to make a joke of it.

'Dear Jeannie,' he said one day, 'we've moved out of the magic-lantern age.'

Jeannie, therefore, had to be convinced that the market required daffodils in the form of grass, and the first step was to prove a pencil-sharp bud would eventually turn into a daffodil. The second depended on the price returns we received during the course of the season. We would have to wait for the result of the latter but, after a week, we knew the response of the bud in the jar. After a few days the bud began to nod away from the stem, then came a suspicion of yellow and, finally, after over a week, the Magnificence bud turned into a daffodil.

I was on my way to prove the worth of my commercial views, but Jeannie had the last word:

'It isn't a genuine, naturally grown daffodil.'

'Agreed,' was my reply, 'but if we want to get the best prices, that's the way we have to send them.'

She looked sad.

'Flowers,' she said, 'have become accountancy units.'

EIGHT

'Be careful . . . so easy to cut yourself.'

Quiet over Christmas, quiet over the New Year, quiet to within a week of marketing the first daffodils, and then a gale.

'Be careful . . .'

Jeannie's advice was sensible, obvious in fact, but I too had to be sensible; and as the gale blew, as glass shuddered, cracked, opened up gaps in a greenhouse, allowing the wind to sweep in, to churn inside, providing the opportunity to create the damage of a miniature cyclone, I could not stand by and watch.

'Be careful . . .'

And I went outside with her words in my ears and the gale in my face, coming from the east, from the Lizard, coming viciously across Mount's Bay.

I had to be sensible. I could not let the capital we had sunk into the greenhouses disappear just because I had to be careful. I had to try to save them. I had to plug the gaps of broken glass. I had to take risks.

Modern technology had lessened the risks. When the greenhouses had been erected, the only way to plug a broken glass panel was with a new one, and who could carry a five feet by two feet section of glass in a gale and fit it into position? But now there was polythene; rolls of polythene like rolls of carpet, which I cut into the appropriate size, and then endeavoured to fix into position, fix into the gap caused by the broken glass, I tried to fix as the gale blew.

It was now that I missed the presence of Geoffrey, missed the presence of someone who was born to the art of practical work. No trouble for them. The ladder would have been placed in a safe position, the polythene would have been cut the exact size, miraculously it would have been held under control as the stapling machine punched it fast to the wooden frame; no difficulty at all. But me . . . the ladder seemed insecure, the polythene, despite my careful endeavour to cut it to size, was never cut to size, one end was too narrow and the other end too wide, and the stapling machine in my hand would get stuck, no staple would come out as I stood on the insecure ladder, with the five feet by two feet piece of polythene blowing like a kite in the gale.

The gale, and there were other gales before the winter was out, was nothing compared with the gale that blew for three days in a year from this time; but it was frightening enough. Yet, as I floundered with the polythene, I was being educated as to the minuses and pluses of working on your own after long being accustomed to assistance.

I had found, for instance, how surprising it was that so much work, hitherto delegated, could be done by oneself. It is, of course, a common discovery. One result of high wages, high prices, high inflation, is that so many of us have found in ourselves hidden talents. Up to a few years ago the do-it-yourself brigade was confined to those who treated such work as a hobby, while the rest of us considered it a tiresome time-waster.

But today . . . well, one can spend the morning painting a room in the house, treat oneself to a bottle of wine at lunch, and still have £18 of unpaid-out wages to spare. Thus, inflation has produced a reason for being a handyman. One is handsomely rewarded. The work involved is no longer a tiresome time-waster, and a handyman of quality is among the elite. Indeed, if I were young, if I were wooing a girl, if I were trying to gain a one-upmanship point over a rival, I would take a course in home decorating and home repairs. Any man, whether film star, tycoon, golf champion, Whitehall clerk, or Olympic Games competitor, who can tell a girl that he can do anything about the house from building a book case to repairing the plumbing, must be irresistible.

Unfortunately for Jeannie, I am not such a man. True, I have my moments and sometimes achieve some task which, beforehand, I feared was beyond my capability, but this does not happen very often. I seem to lack the ability to concentrate on detail. It is a weakness that has always been with me. I was never one, for instance, who was able to pass those tests which psychologists set to judge a person's intelligence. Fortunately, when my career began, such tests were rare. An industry had not been built around them. It followed, that a young man like myself, lacking in conventional ability, had the chance to win a job because the interviewer relied on his hunch. For my part, I would never be writing this book, or have written any books, had it not been for the then young Max Aitken of the *Daily Express*. I had an interview with him at a time when I was an out-of-work clerk with a burning wish to become a journalist. We talked, he asked questions, and he decided to back me by proposing I go to Manchester on trial. Had he, however, as would happen today, asked me what degrees I held, whether I had passed some journalistic training course, then sent me into the next room to wrestle with the psychologists' tests . . . I would have remained an out-of-work clerk.

One of my moments, one of those moments when I achieved a task which, beforehand, I feared was beyond my capability, concerned the refurbishing of our two garden tables and four garden chairs. They were of elaborately-designed ironwork. Every year, each spring, we regretted that during the winter we had not arranged for these garden necessities to be repainted, and our regrets were due to the ever-increasing rust marks which appeared on both chairs and tables. At last, I asked for an estimate for repairs and the answer came that the refurbishing would cost more than I had paid for the chairs and the tables in the first place.

This information set me on a pattern of action that appealed to my weakness for gadgets, and I became one of the thousands who own an electric drill with accessories, and one of the accessories was a wire-brush with which I proceeded to flake off the rust and the paint on the garden chairs and tables. First the chairs, then the tables and, after each one had been flaked, I stood back and admired my achievement. And if Jeannie were nearby, I would call her. 'Marvellous,' she would say, staring at the now rustless ironwork. And when, later, I had completed the painting, first a primer, then two coats of white gloss, and the chairs and the tables looked as if they were new, there was further self-admiration, further requests by me for praise from Jeannie. It was not vanity, however, which required this admiration. It was a question of reassurance, a counter to my lack of confidence. I am one of those people who is always looking for reassurance, even when refurbishing four garden chairs and two tables.

One is born, I suppose, with a lack of self-confidence, for no reasoning can expel its mood. Some conduct their lives as if they have never had any doubt as to their abilities, creating an aura around themselves which earns a respect that is undeserved; and there are, of course, those whose self-confidence *is* deserved, who sweep through life with élan, never doubting their talents, and these are the lucky ones. As for myself, born with a lack of self-confidence, I belong to the group who shout in the dark, who sometimes brashly pretend the fates are on their side or, in contrast, yield too easily to opposition . . . but the undercurrent is always the same. One is yearning for encouragement to banish the doubts.

My attitude towards women, for instance, has seldom fulfilled the ideal I would have liked it to have been. I had a monastic childhood, and the first girl to whom I ever desired to pay attention I met one summer when I was on holiday with my parents in the coast town of Knocke in Belgium.

I was fifteen, and a dance band played during dinner each evening at the hotel where we stayed. While I sat at a table on one side of the dance floor with my parents, a young French girl sat at a table on the other side with her mother. Two evenings passed by with my interest growing and, on the third, dinner over, coffee cups on the table, courage suddenly in my hands, I said to my parents that I was going to walk across the dance floor and invite this girl to dance with me. It was a period when the formality of introduction was expected, and my parents gently tried to dissuade me, no doubt fearing a rebuff. There was no rebuff. I bowed to the mother at the table; I bowed to the girl, and she rose, and we danced, and were happy. Then I saw out of the corner of my eye my father and mother, heads together, watching us, laughing, and I realised that, loving me as they did, they felt embarrassed that I was showing interest in a girl and this made me feel self-conscious. I lost my confidence and felt foolish, and stumbled in my dance-steps, and the girl's magic faded away.

This juvenile incident must have had some effect on my attitude towards women, since it has haunted me through the years; and I have watched, like an outsider, the incident being repeated in various forms. Timidity is the factor. I should have ignored the well-meaning antics of my parents on that evening at Knocke, should have taken charge of the situation and asked the girl to dance again, and again, but instead I allowed myself to feel foolish, feel scared of being laughed at, and so surrendered my role as a suitor. Women, I was to learn, prefer to be led, not followed.

I was not, however, timid when I met Jeannie. I was, she says, aggressive. We were introduced in the foyer of the Savoy Hotel, and I had a one-track mind about a book that had just been published, my first ever, called *Time was Mine*, a travel diary of a journey I had made round the world. My sense of opportunism realised that this slim girl, who, despite her youth, was publicity officer of the Savoy, could be a key figure in the success of the book. She knew everyone of importance in the journalistic, radio, film and theatre world, and so if she could become a convert to the book she could be the kind of ally that authors yearn for. Moreover, and this prompted my immediate interest in her, she had influence as to the contents of the Savoy Hotel bookstall. Thus, when we were introduced, I in my uniform as a Captain in the Intelligence Corps, and she in a black skirt and white silk shirt, with a waist around which a pair of hands would meet, I, without any hesitation, said, 'Will you get my book on the bookstall?' She did.

My aggressive beginning quickly mellowed. Jeannie was surrounded by fascinating men, war correspondents of world renown, pilots, film stars touring war zones, all of whom, I observed, loved her. She was balm for such people in those days. All values are relative and so it might be said that stresses of today are equal to the stresses of war years, any war years. But this is not true. Jeannie cared for people living on borrowed time, English, French, Polish, American; and she saw that when they came to the Savoy their fantasy dreams came true. And when the war correspondents arrived from some theatre of war of which they wished they had never been a part, it was Jeannie who saw they received the hotel attention they needed. She was conscious, without any sense of dramatics, that any one of them she might not see again.

An American magazine was to describe her as the 'prettiest press officer in the world', and there was no doubt that this was true. But, at this period, my interest in her, my courting of her among so much competition, had also a practical side to it. I was in charge of a special M.I.5 section which had a wide-ranging mandate that included monitoring the mood of people in influential circles, collecting rumours that could be passed on to the German High Command as fact via double agents, vetting individuals and conducting various other activities which were related to the Secret Service. I also had two weekly meetings . . . one with the heads of M.I.5, the other with the Secretary of the War Cabinet. Any information

I considered of importance, or any viewpoint that I believed was being blocked by red tape, was passed on by me at these Monday meetings and, in the case of the Secretary of the War Cabinet, passed straight on to Number 10. None of the people I met at the Savoy, or anywhere else, was aware of my role. I was just a harmless Captain in the Intelligence Corps who had joined in the race for Jean Nicol, as Jeannie was called at the time.

Unsuspected by her, however, she gradually became an important link in the chain of my work. Through her I was able to meet many people of contemporary importance by the simple method of being in her company, or joining her in the Savoy Bar, and frequently she would innocently pass on to me items of interest. Items which had nothing to do with Secret Service work, but were concerning the war effort, concerning perhaps the frustration of an influential American war correspondent who was being thwarted from obtaining a permit to do this or that. She would tell me of the frustration, or he himself would tell me as he sat with us in the Bar and, within a week, he would have his desired permit.

Jeannie, therefore, had become of dual importance to me. Romantically I was chasing her; Secret Service-wise I needed her, and so it was with some concern that she announced one evening she had been called up and that she had been summoned to attend the Call-Up Office in Denmark Street in the West End next day.

'I'm not worrying,' she said, the *New York Times* correspondent on one side of her on the sofa in the Bar, the *Time Magazine* correspondent on the other, 'Mr Wontner has written such a strong letter saying I'm better employed here . . .' and then she paused, '. . . I think I'm not worrying.'

Mr Wontner, now Sir Hugh Wontner, was Chairman of the Savoy, Claridge's and Berkeley Company, and was already one of the most influential men in the hotel world. Today, he is the doyen.

'I'm taking the letter with me tomorrow,' Jeannie added.

'You're certain to be OK,' said the *New York Times* man.

'I'll meet you here for a drink to celebrate tomorrow evening,' said the man from *Time Magazine*.

There was no celebration.

I was there when Jeannie arrived back from Denmark Street and she described how she had been interviewed by a fierce lady, by a lady who had read Hugh Wontner's letter, dismissed it as irrelevant, and when Jeannie, realising the inevitable, asked if she could be called up in the Wrens, replied: 'The ATS for you! No protest about that!'

I said nothing. I left the Savoy soon afterwards and went back to Richmond, where I then lived, and the following afternoon I rang Jeannie and suggested a drink around six o'clock. When she arrived, she greeted me ecstatically, which obviously pleased me.

'They've had second thoughts! . . . After all, I am to stay here!'

I expressed my delight, but I did not immediately tell her how the 'second thoughts' had been arrived at, how my chief had agreed with me that she would be far more useful at the Savoy than marching with the ATS. I have often wondered what the fierce lady of the Denmark Street Call-Up Office must have thought when she was ordered to 'forget' her new recruit.

'Be careful . . . so easy to cut yourself.'

Her words had guarded me as I floundered with the polythene, struggling to hold it in position long enough to staple it on the frame that had held the smashed glass. They guarded me to such an extent that I soon realised I was risking unnecessary danger. Why not be prudent? Why risk being slashed to save a greenhouse? And so it was that, not long after I had set out on my polythene mission, I was back in the cottage.

'Thank goodness,' said Jeannie. 'I didn't want to interfere . . . but I thought you were crazy.'

I suppose I should hate gales. They have done enough

damage to us in our time. Potato crops ruined, daffodils flattened, garden plants blackened, summer leaves of the trees turned brown, and always the threat of smashed glass. But I find there is a certain comfort in the fury of a gale, a kind of antidote to the artificial standards of our civilisation. Here we are in this period of technical brilliance, a period in which scientists aim to conquer the natural forces of nature, in which academic doctrines lead us to believe that all will be well with our lives if we follow the rules they expound for marriage, for health, for social problems, a period in which standardisation has become the Nirvana, a period in which we are fooled into thinking that there can be fair shares for all . . . and along comes a gale. It lashes the land and boils the sea, turning ships into cockleshells, mocking man's conceit, reminding us as we listen to its roar that man-made theories do not control us, that nature remains supreme. I find solace in a gale. I find solace despite the fact I am scared of the damage it might do. I still find solace . . . despite the gale, as I will later tell, that scythed through Minack a year later.

After a gale, after twelve hours of fury, after twenty-four hours, sometimes after forty-eight hours, when there is silence instead of a din like a multitude of rushing tube trains, and I can hear again the cooing of pigeons in the wood, and the donkeys come out from the shelter of the stable, and a gull settles on the roof, and Oliver and Ambrose stroll unperturbed down the lane, I will take a walk and assess the damage that has been done.

On this occasion, besides a half dozen panes of smashed glass, a section of the garage roof had been blown away.

The word garage is, however, too superior for the place. When we first came to Minack there were various shadows of long ago buildings in the neighbourhood of the cottage: outlines of stone walls smothered by under-growth, a ghost world of pig-sties, farm-implement shelters, and sheds where long-forgotten cows were milked. But the largest shadow of a building was where we now have the garage.

It is not a normal garage. It was created by Tommy Williams, a tall Cornishman, dark and wiry, with flashing eyes and the manner of an evangelist, who helped us at the beginning of our time at Minack. Tommy had a visionary's view of the world, declaiming how standards of honesty would deteriorate, how if you believe in freedom you must not envy the good luck of others, how the pre-war generation faced always with the threat of death were more aware of basic happiness, how too much time is spent arguing about the mechanics of living instead of getting on with living, how the quiet of Cornwall would be taken over by philistines whose only interest was to exploit it . . . I would listen to him declaiming his views as we planted potatoes in the cliff, Tommy pausing to rest his hands on the end of his long-handled shovel, staring out to sea, and me, wanting him to get on with his job of shovelling the ground as I dropped the potato seed behind him. He had the stature of a primitive prophet, a madness which made him misunderstood, and Jeannie and I would listen and be aware that we were hearing the voice of Cornwall. A voice that would mean nothing to many who came to Cornwall. Tommy to them would have been a comical yokel. For only the sensitive from across the Tamar understood the mysticism of the Cornish.

Tommy Williams looked at the shadow of the building which was to become our garage, and rejoiced that it gave him the opportunity to make use of his love of stone. You see the results of his labours today, and they are unconventional. Some of the stones, rocks in fact, were far too large for him to remove, and there they are bulging into the garage from an earth bank which serves as one side of the garage. But it was the roof which now concerned me, for a large part of it was open to the sky, the gale had whipped the boards away and one glance told me that repairing it would be a major job, an expensive one.

I was not, however, as concerned about the lack of weather protection the car would now receive as I was about Oliver and Ambrose . . . and the swallows. The car, a Volvo Estate, which carried our daffodil boxes in spring, our tomato boxes in summer, serving us as if it were a van, had such a high standard of weather-proof protection on the chassis that no harm would come to it. Harm, on the other hand, could come to Oliver and Ambrose.

Oliver and Ambrose, throughout the year, enjoyed sprawling on the garage roof for, on a morning when the sun was shining and the wind was a westerly, they could bask there with the trees sheltering them. It was a flat roof and they also liked to use it as a look out point at night. I have often seen them up there, peering over the side, observing movements of mice or whatever below them, my torch momentarily lighting them up and thereby vexing them.

But now there was a hole in the roof. Supposing they did not see it as they prowled at night? Supposing, being over-familiar with the roof, they took it for granted that all was well? The prospect fed me with my customary neurotic fears. I visioned them plummeting from the roof, having walked into space. My imagination saw broken paws, even a broken back. As a result, before I patched up any more broken panes of glass, I patched up the space in the roof. Three narrow pieces of wood were laid across it. Traffic lights, so to speak, giving Oliver and Ambrose a warning that something was amiss.

Our concern about the swallows, on the other hand, was not immediate. It was due to the fact that a couple of years ago they changed their nesting venue from the stables where the donkeys had their headquarters, to the garage, and each year they had two broods; each year two mud-made nests miraculously fastened to one of the beams which supported the roof. The beams were still there, but now this gap in the roof; and I, with one of those weird anticipations of things to come, foresaw that the repairing of the roof would be put off and put off, for one reason or another, until suddenly I would be faced with the imminent arrival of the swallows at Minack, and no roof. But there was still plenty of time. Our pair of swallows were still sweeping around the skies of South Africa, not a thought of the journey to summer England yet in their minds.

Our immediate problem, however, revolved around the tight buds of the daffodils. I may have persuaded Jeannie in theory that the sending of tight buds was the policy of the future, but the time had now come to put the theory to the practical test. I foresaw stalling on her part. She, I feared, who had taken such pride over the years in packing the daffodils, would revolt when she began packing the buds that resembled grass. But first we had to pick them, and the maiden picking took place a few days after the gale had abated.

This maiden picking had become an annual ritual, involving Oliver and Ambrose, a quiet beginning in contrast to the rush ahead of us, a stroll from meadow to meadow down Minack cliff, picking a few Magnificence from one meadow, a few from another, and all the while Oliver and Ambrose would follow us. It was an erratic way of picking daffodils for market. The venture began, on this occasion, by taking Fred and Merlin away from the stable field where they had spent the night, up by their halters past the cottage and into the big field which is above the cottage. They were not very pleased by our action. They were clearly in the mood for a walk and they would have preferred us to have taken them up the lane, taken them to the top of the hill, and beyond. But we had to remove them from the stable field for the sake of Oliver and Ambrose. Had they observed Oliver and Ambrose following us as we set off with our daffodil baskets, they would have wished to come too.

Thus we set off down the path alongside the stable field to the white gate (so chewed by the donkeys that by the time you read this there may be a new one), into the field where Fred was born, then down the track to the top of Minack cliff. We arrived at the small gate which tops the cliff while Oliver and Ambrose were many yards behind us, diverted by movements real or imaginary, in the matting of grass which bordered the track. I called them and they took no notice. Then, in order to display our own independence, we opened the gate and walked down the steps to the first meadow. Immediately, we heard miaows from way up the track behind us. Annoyed miaows, as if the message was: 'Wait for us! *Wait for us!*'

It was a crisp day, flaky clouds in the sky, and a breeze ruffling the sea. A few miles offshore, two massive deep-sea trawlers, curse of the local fishermen, patrolled slowly westwards, their fishing gear sucking up fish like a vacuum cleaner. In Mount's Bay, to the east, was anchored a Dutch tug, waiting for news of some vessel in distress to which it could rush, like a spider waiting for a fly to be caught in its web. Around us on the cliff was tranquillity. Yellow flecks of winter gorse, the pleasant scent of young nettles, dog violets showing between the rows of the daffodil beds, the occasional primrose in bloom before its time, waves below us swaying against the rocks, their foam like Cornish cream, and suddenly a flight of curlews veering momentarily out to sea when they saw us, then on eastwards towards Lamorna, calling their magical cries.

'Why, I wonder,' I said to Jeannie, 'whenever I see a flight of curlews is there always one apart from the rest?'

'There are probably loners even among curlews,' she answered, her mind half with me only, because Oliver and Ambrose had just appeared at our feet.

'Honoured we are,' said Jeannie, bending down to stroke Ambrose, who immediately jumped away, jumped towards Oliver, wanting a game, wanting to play hide and seek among the green leaves of the daffodils.

The meadows of Minack cliff are steep, so when you pick, you pick upwards not downwards; you pick until you reach the top of the meadow, and then you walk down and start again, and the meadows are small. They are far too small for modern standards of cultivation. The bulbs cannot be lifted as purists would like them to be lifted. All we can do is to cut the undergrowth away in the autumn and let the bulbs produce their flowers naturally. Costs have eliminated proper care. Costs, in fact, have eliminated the use of almost all the cliff meadows, except ours, between Penzance and Land's End, once a prized area of early growing. Yet our bulbs still flourish and there we were that morning, Oliver and Ambrose gambolling, doing something with the daffodils we had never done before. We were picking them as grass.

Not quite.

'This is the way we are supposed to pick them . . . look.'

And I held up a Magnificence, held up a stem and the bud, so that it appeared like a green pencil.

'Oh no,' groaned Jeannie.

'It's how they want it . . .'

'Sorry, I can't agree.'

'But you must . . . Ben Green and Russ insisted . . . and you know that our experimental bud came out.'

Ben and Russ are the remarkable couple who organise the produce sales of the Society of Growers through which we market our daffodils.

'I think,' said Jeannie, 'that this is the sort of daffodil we should pick . . . experimental bud notwithstanding.'

And she held up a Magnificence with just a touch of yellow showing from its calyx.

As she did so, Oliver detached himself from the game he was supposed to be playing with Ambrose, and began rubbing his head against my leg, purring, and the pleasure of the moment diverted me from my business-like outlook, for I said:

'Jeannie, darling, I'll agree with you this time. If I were wooing you, the last thing I would do is to hope to excite you with a bunch of grass.'

'So let's pick the daffodil buds with just a little yellow showing.'

'For the sake of the wooers.'

'That's right.'

We went our leisurely way, picking the type of buds Jeannie wanted to pick, and sometimes we had to call Oliver and Ambrose to join us. Sometimes they pretended they were lost and they shouted their miaows; and sometimes they were under our feet, apparently so full of sudden love for us that they expected, without question, that we should surrender our task of picking the daffodil buds in favour of relaxing with them. We were happy to do so. We were in no rush.

We meandered on, choosing buds with the calyx just breaking, pausing, looking out to sea, watching Oliver take a flying leap on to the branch of an elder tree, breathing the salty air of the sea, until at last we had covered the meadows and a basket was full, and it was time to return to the cottage and bunch. No problem this time about Oliver and Ambrose following us. They raced up the track, came to a stop until we caught up with them, and then raced away again. They never seemed to like to be away from Minack for long. They were never wandering cats.

We had enough buds to fill two daffodil boxes, forty-five bunches in each box, ten buds in each bunch and when, before putting the lids on, we looked at the neatly packed rows, just a touch of yellow showing from most of the buds, we felt confident that we had picked them at the right stage. They looked like grass, true enough, but at least there was a hint of yellow.

We were wrong.

From the salesman in Covent Garden to whom we had sent the two boxes came a message with the invoice a few days later. Just two words:

'Too open.'

NINE

Too open . . .

From that moment, the moment the invoice arrived, we debated the matter no further.

We surrendered.

'If they want grass, they will have to have grass.'

'Poor wooers,' said Jeannie.

'Never mind the wooers.'

She looked pensive.

'What are you thinking about?'

'I was thinking,' she replied, 'of errant husbands arriving home late for dinner with a bunch of grass in their hands.'

'What an absurd thought,' I said, laughing.

'I remember you coming home late one night when we were at Mortlake, and your apology present caught me completely by surprise.'

'What was it?'

'An "A" subscription to Harrods' library.'

'You were delighted.'

'I know . . . I forgave you for spoiling the dinner. How do you think I would have reacted if you had brought me a bunch of grass?'

'I don't dare to imagine.'

'That's my point.'

'Heavens, Jeannie,' I said, 'we're not in business for errant husbands.'

She laughed.

'Come on, let's go and pick some more grass.'

Clearly, Jeannie and I thought that we were doing a disservice to the public for the sake of commercial gain. But on the day of our final decision to send grass, we received a letter from Carlo Naef, doyen of flower salesmen, Italian born, elegant as a professional diplomat, and dedicated to the promotion of Scillonian and Cornish daffodils. He had the air of a man you can trust, a quiet assurance which made one believe that what he said would inevitably come to pass.

One year, the day after the end of the annual Spring Flower Show at Penzance, at which he was a judge, he came to lunch with us, and along with him came his old friend Phyllis Whale. Mrs Whale, a small, alert person, was spoken of in the flower-growing community in the same awed tone of voice as one might speak of a leading dancer in the Royal Ballet, and we first met her when we intended to grow several thousand wallflower plants early on in our time at Minack. We were advised to contact her, as she was known as the wallflower queen in growing circles, and the contact led to friendship and, over the years, we regularly called on her.

She lived at Coverack, her home within spray distance of the sea, and in sight of the original Lizard Lifeboat Station. She was in her nineties when we last called upon her there, knocking tentatively on her glass-panelled front door and receiving our usual welcome from her.

'Come in, my dears, have a drink, I've been given a bottle of gin.' Then, adding hurriedly, 'The 2.30 at Ascot is just about to be off. . . I've backed the second favourite.' And Jeannie and I would hasten into the sitting room and share the punter's excitement in front of the television set.

Phyllis Whale was revered too by the salesmen of Covent Garden. She had standards. Every bloom she sent away to market, violets, of which she was at one time the largest grower in the county, daffodils, wallflowers, polyanthus, anemones, agapanthus, all had superb quality.

Each bloom a perfection; each box exquisitely packed. That long time ago, when Jeannie and I were advised to contact her, proved to be our very special good fortune. She was always fun to be with and there was always much to learn from her about flowers.

The letter from Carlo Naef outlined the reasons why daffodils should be marketed as grass, or, in the official phrase, in the 'hard pencil stage'. Since he was the head of J. and E. Page, the wholesalers in Covent Garden to whom we sent most of our flowers, he was someone to whom one should listen, as a schoolboy might listen to a headmaster. He was adamant that daffodils should be sent in the hard pencil stage. He enclosed with his letter a copy of an article he had written in which he quoted Peter Barr, a noted daffodil specialist, who in 1884 urged Scillonian daffodil growers whose daffodil programme was then in its infancy, to market their daffodils in tight bud. And Peter Barr added: 'Flower buds cut in this way open fresher and attain a larger size than would have been the case had they remained uncut.'

Brave words in 1884, though it seems strange that it took until the 1970s before such a custom of picking daffodils became a habit. Of course, in the meantime, vast glasshouses have been erected in this country in which millions of bulbs are forced by heat and have to be quickly cleared, and to pick them in the hard pencil stage is one way of doing so. Thus one might wonder whether the glasshouse daffodil industry has provoked this love affair with the hard pencil stage. I have seen their offerings on the stands of Covent Garden and have been shocked. I could not imagine who would buy the wafer-thin stalks. When buying early spring daffodils, therefore, ask the florist whether the daffodils are outside grown, Cornish or Scillonian. The Cornish and the Scillonian daffodils, although in the hard pencil stage, have firm stalks as they have grown up naturally towards the sky. They have not been artificially pampered, like battery hens.

Whatever our feelings, I have to confess that the new way of sending was profitable. We realised, as the season unfolded, that we were heading for the best daffodil season ever. There were various reasons for this. The weather was cold, for one thing. Nothing hinders a daffodil season more than a warm spring in which the sun brings the daffodils into bud so fast that you cannot catch up with them, and they have to be left unpicked, soon turning the meadows into a sequence of yellow lakes.

And the other reason was that we found it *was* so much quicker to pick in the hard pencil stage and to bunch and to pack. All through the season, through February and March, we knew we were on top of our work, on top of being able to send every possible daffodil away, and there were only the three of us. Jeannie, Margaret and myself. Margaret the potter, who lives at the end of our lane, whose enthusiasm, whose willingness to work in all weathers (and picking for three hours in a gale and rain is tough), helped to make this rush period so pleasant and exciting and worthwhile.

Mingoose Merlin, on the other hand, did not view the situation in the same fashion. Nor did Fred, for that matter. Nor did Oliver and Ambrose. The routines of all four were turned topsy-turvy. For instance, there was no lying in bed for Oliver and Ambrose in the morning. They normally like to take their time in getting up, spreading themselves across our legs, or Oliver might settle himself on my chest, or Ambrose might so arrange himself that he curled up alongside Jeannie, often purring at full throttle. Fortunately, we had no timetable to follow, no commuter train to catch, though we had our consciences to worry about. It was wrong to be influenced by sleepy cats. It was wrong to lie there, dozing when we had work to do. But we did doze, and we did hesitate to move a leg or an arm in case of upsetting the sleepy cats and we did, therefore, deserve the rebukes of all practical people who, in similar circumstances, would have pushed the sleepy cats off the bed. The clock in the sitting room, the clock that stands on the oak chest, given to Jeannie by the Savoy Hotel directors as a leaving present, would chime eight o'clock . . .

117

'It's slow,' Jeannie would murmur from the pillow. 'I know it's slow . . . it must be a quarter past.'

Sometimes in these moments of doziness, I would have total recall of icy mornings at Harrow School, when two minutes of extra time in bed before the compulsory cold bath and a run to the classroom was heaven.

'*You* put on the kettle . . .'

Jeannie was awakening.

Silence from me.

'Go on, you're nearest.'

True enough. Our bedroom is so absurdly small that for Jeannie to get round the bed and into the sitting room is like following a miniature steeplechase course. All I, however, had to do was to get out of bed, walk a couple of yards, and I was in the galley of a kitchen, able to light the gas for the kettle.

But there was Oliver . . .

'Oliver is on my chest,' I murmured back to Jeannie.

'Go on, push him off.'

'How cruel.'

In due course, I would slither out of bed, gently leaving Oliver, set the kettle on to boil and the day would quietly begin.

Not so during the daffodil season.

We were brisk in the morning during the daffodil season. The alarm was set at six, and there was no dozing, no pandering to sleepy cats. Oliver on my chest; Ambrose curled beside Jeannie; no matter, both were unceremoniously pushed away. That this treatment annoyed them, only F people would understand, just as F people would also understand that we ourselves were upset by inflicting it on them. Non-F people, on the other hand, would deride us. Yet I have found, over the years, that those who are tender about the feelings of animals, any animals, are those who are most likely to be sensitive to the feelings of human beings. In a personal, individual way.

We did not, however, allow any sensitivity to interfere with the progress of the daffodil season, and so Oliver and Ambrose discovered other aspects of their lives were disturbed. They enjoyed, during non-daffodil time, to sleep often in the small greenhouse where we bunched and packed the daffodils. This is the greenhouse where nothing is grown, where there is a cement floor and long benches are on either side of its interior. It is a storeroom housing a multitude of odds and ends for most of the year but, in summer, it is used for the weighing and packing of tomatoes and, in the spring, for bunching and packing daffodils. It was only in daffodil time that Oliver and Ambrose fled from it . . . except when we had finished bunching, then they would return and lie among the flower tins.

Fred, the previous year, had special privileges during the daffodil season. He was on his own, Penny had died and we had set out to console him by letting him have a freedom that, in normal times, would have been denied him. We let him wander around the environment of the cottage without a halter, walk up the lane without a halter, let him munch grass in the small orchard, and even when he demolished two young plum trees we reacted as if he had done no worse than consume a bramble. And when the daffodil season began in earnest, he was allowed to accompany us as we picked. He would walk delicately up the rows and, surprisingly, he would avoid trampling on the blooms. As we stooped, picking, he would sometimes come up behind one of us, nudging us; and he showed a special liking for Margaret and the brown woolly hat she wore. She would be busily picking and be suddenly aware of a donkey's nose rubbing against her head. 'Fred,' she would call out, 'you're after my hat again!'

This season there was no chance of such freedom. Fred might behave in sedate fashion on his own, but there was no chance of such good behaviour in the company of Mingoose Merlin. Merlin, I had no difficulty in realising, would treat a meadow of daffodils in the same way he would treat a field, scampering over it, luring Fred to chase him, treating the whole situation while we picked as an opportunity to frolic. Merlin, long-haired Merlin, whom Jeannie sometimes would say looked like a yak, sometimes like a clown, was not the sort of donkey one could trust. He was looking for fun. He would not take seriously our task of picking daffodils for market. Hence Fred had to suffer. He had to surrender the freedom he had enjoyed during the daffodil time of the previous year, and to enjoy instead, as compensation, the constant company of Merlin.

Merlin, since he arrived at Minack, had been developing various special interests. One of these interests concerned the interior of the cottage. Since it is a small cottage, the size of a normal town flat, the presence of a donkey inside it provokes anxiety. A lamp may be knocked over, a vase of flowers, china ornaments or photographs standing on the oak chest. All these were in danger when Merlin decided to enter the cottage; and he decided to enter each time I was supposed to be leading him from the donkey field, which is above the cottage, down to the stable field or meadow, which is below the cottage. As we passed the short path leading to the porch, he would tug at the halter, leading me towards the porch. Once there, he would walk in through the door as if he were walking into a stable.

Of course, it was my responsibility that he performed this party trick. I could have held on to the halter. I could have pulled him away. But, in the pre-daffodil time, when there was no hurry to the day, I found his desire to look around the sitting room irresistible. He would walk up to my kidney-shaped Regency desk and push his nose into the untidy pile of papers that lay on it, and he would have a look at the wastepaper basket and momentarily think it contained fodder to eat. There was no hint of clumsiness in his behaviour, only his inquisitiveness was the danger.

Meanwhile, Fred would stay at the door, his head peering into the porch, making whinnying noises, wondering what Merlin was up to, wishing to join him, but scared that his bulk would cause problems if he did so. A two-year-old might be at ease investigating the inside of a cottage, but not a grown up donkey like himself. I think, too, that he was jealous of Merlin; jealous of the attention that Merlin was receiving out of sight of him. Like the moment when Merlin put his head into our galley of a kitchen.

'Merlin!' cried Jeannie, 'Get out of my kitchen!'

A wail of whinnying notes from the porch.

'Merlin!'

Merlin had seen newly-baked buns on a plate.

More whinnying notes from the porch.

'Go away, Merlin . . . you're not going to have one here. I'll give you one with Fred outside.'

There was no problem in turning him away. A push on his head to set him in the right direction, a push on his posterior, and Merlin walked out of the sitting room into the porch and outside to join Fred. And then both were rewarded with buns.

But no such diversions during the daffodil season; no time for dallying; no time for walks; no time for the game that Merlin liked me playing with him . . . that of wrapping a matchbox in my handkerchief and chasing

121

him round the field, the rattling matches spurring him to run away from me at great speed. Instead, he would stand by the gate of the field he was in and watch us hastening by on our tasks. Fred would watch too, balefully. Both disliked the daffodil season. They disliked being ignored.

Their ostracism lasted throughout February and the first week of March and, by then, the yellows were over, the yellow daffodils, and there was an interval of a couple of weeks before the whites began, and during that couple of weeks comfortable routines were restored, and Fred and Merlin were content again; so too were Oliver and Ambrose.

Unfortunately for us, fortunately for them, our need to ignore them was never resumed. The best yellow daffodil season we had enjoyed was followed by the failure of the whites. These whites, as the white narcissi crop is broadly known, all flowered profusely . . . Barrett Browning, Early Bride, Brunswick, Actaea . . . but the whites everywhere flowered profusely, and they also happened to coincide with a glut of Lincolnshire field-yellow daffodils. This all added up to a glut in the market.

The glut caught us by surprise. Gluts always do. It is a penalty of not having a telephone. We refuse to have a telephone because we find that an ingredient for enjoying a country life is to try to live it as it was lived in time past; and in time past there was no ringing bell to interrupt the day, no threat of a ringing bell. When we lived in London it was very different. I was a telephone king, and Jeannie was a telephone queen. Hours were spent gossiping, which often meant saying things one should not have said, and regretting them later; or accepting invitations which, if they had come by letter, one would have had time to reflect upon and refuse; or, more dangerously, seizing the telephone because some event had made one indignant. We were now spared such hazards. We were spared those anxiety questions: 'Will you answer it?' or 'Has anyone rung?' And the penalty we had to pay for such tranquillity was, momentarily, to be unaware of the glut.

Had we a telephone, I would have rung up Russ or Ben Green of the Society of Growers at their headquarters at Long Rock outside Penzance, and they would have told me of the market situation. Instead, by seven in the morning, Jeannie and I were out amongst the Actaea crop and picking as fast as we could, delighted the crop was so plentiful. Soon after breakfast, Margaret joined us and the three of us continued to pick, filling the wicker baskets with Actaea until we knew we had as many as we could bunch and pack before I drove them to Penzance Station to catch the afternoon flower train to take them to Covent Garden.

'I'll start picking again while you're away,' said Jeannie.

Margaret was coming with me to her cottage at the end of the lane and in the back were twenty boxes of Actaea, sixty bunches in each, and if the price was fair they would fetch £100 after paying the cost of the freight, commission and the price of the boxes.

'I'll try and finish what we left this morning,' added Jeannie.

You have to have enthusiasm and stamina to pick for long periods. Jeannie had both.

'I'll be at least an hour,' I said. 'I'll go up to Long Rock after the station and find out what the market is like.'

I went to Long Rock after putting the boxes on the train and saw Russ and I was away for longer than an hour because roadworks held me up on the way there and on the way back, and all the while I was thinking of Jeannie picking away, and how she would be trying to finish the Actaea and so give me pleasure on my return.

I drew up the Volvo in front of the cottage just as she was walking back through the orchard.

'Done it!' she called out, happily, 'two full baskets for you to collect!'

I did not dither.

'It's no good . . . the price is on the floor.'

'Oh, no.'

She stood still.

'Russ says we'll be lucky if today's sending is sold at all . . . and certainly it's pointless to send any more.'

She had worked so hard and so fast.

'Never mind,' I said, 'they're not wasted. The hospital will love them.'

And the daffodil season was over.

The tomato plants came that week and the winds came too. In the days of Geoffrey, we had three thousand plants and we had heat, and every ten days the oil lorry would come rumbling down the lane and fill up the tanks. The stink of the burning oil would pervade soft evenings, and I used to worry whether the nesting birds were being affected by the fumes. The tomato plants, in those days, governed our summers, compelling Geoffrey and ourselves to spend hours every day, every weekend, cosseting them. Little came out of it. Perhaps just enough to cover expenses and to pay Geoffrey's wages.

But now we were on our own there was no need to stretch ourselves, foolish if we did so. Heat was out of the question. A lorry-load of oil coming down the lane would mean £300 going out of the bank, and so our heating installations, installed with much excitement and hopeful expectations, stood forlornly in the corner of each greenhouse, rusting. And instead of three thousand tomato plants, we were to have three hundred, and they were to prove quite enough for us to handle.

They were called Maascross, the sweetest flavoured tomato I have ever known, though they are not popular with the big commercial growers. Such growers, in order to make their profit, have to feed the market with what is wanted, and the market required tomatoes of perfect size and shape; flavour is irrelevant. Our plants were grown and delivered to us by Ken Hitchens, whose nursery is just outside Truro. When his black Dormobile filled with plants arrived at Minack I felt, as always, that I was about to take from him his precious family. Such beautiful plants, a rich green, all uniform in height. He helped to carry the cardboard trays in which they stood to the two greenhouses where we were going to plant them and, having done so, he stood for a moment, wistfully looking at them. No wonder. If I had grown such beautiful plants from seed and was now handing them over to the unknown, I would have felt the same.

The winds came again, and they shook the greenhouses, and first one side-glass panel slipped, then another, then another. The glass itself did not break, but the wedge holding a panel in position got loosened and then fell away, and so the panel dropped, leaving a space at the top, which I would go out and plug with a strip of polythene. Or one of the roof panels slipped and this was more tricky to deal with because I had to lean a ladder against the relevant section of the greenhouse, climb up the ladder, and fix the slipping panel by tapping a nail into the frame with a hammer, stretching out over the glass roof, imagining all the time that the ladder might slip and I would crash through the roof.

The winds came, but they were not severe; they did not scare me as the gale, now less than a year hence, was to scare me. The winds blew with determination, but not with rage. The damage they caused was an inconvenience, not a disaster. Far worse winds had attacked the greenhouses before; far worse were to come. But the winds in the week that the tomato plants arrived alerted me, reminding me of my responsibilities to the swallows who were due to arrive again in the garage within a month.

There had been no further damage to the roof since the centre boards had been ripped away, since I had placed the narrow strips of wood across the empty gap as a warning to Oliver and Ambrose, who enjoyed prowling on the roof. Yet, when I now came to examine it more closely, I found weaknesses in other parts of it. It was an unusual flat roof in the sense that, although the sixteen-feet length was uniform, the width was twelve feet at the open end and fourteen feet at the far end and, although one side was held in normal fashion on the stone wall facing the Orlyt, the top side was embedded in the earth bank below the cottage. It was clearly an improvised roof, and so, when I invited a roof expert to have a look at it, inviting him to give me an estimate as to the cost of its repair, the expert gave a snort.

'Don't know how it's lasted so long . . . the wood is rotten . . . look,' and he poked his stick at a plank. 'The wood is soft as sawdust.'

The planks rested across four oak beams.

'The beams are solid enough,' I said, hopefully. Against the beams were still glued the remnants of last summer's two swallow nests.

'You'll have to cut down that climbing rose before any repairs can start,' the expert continued, ignoring my remark. 'And those brambles at the top end, they'll have to go.'

'I understand that.'

The brambles grew out of the bank. The climbing rose, a lovely white rose which began blooming in clusters in June and continued spasmodically to bloom until the autumn, had lodged its tendrils under the felt which covered the roof, prising it up, splitting it in places.

'It's going to be a big job,' said the expert, dubiously. 'Just as well start from scratch.'

'How long do you think it'll take?'

The expert had brought out a ruler and had begun measuring.

'You see,' I added, 'I am anxious about the swallows. They're on the way now from South Africa, and they'll be here in less than a month, and it must be all ready for them when they arrive.'

The expert stopped measuring and turned to me in astonishment.

'Swallows?' he said. 'Do you mean you're doing all this just for swallows?'

'Well, yes, mainly . . . I mean the car is . . .'

'Do you know what it's going to cost?'

'Tell me.'

'A minimum £400!'

I was shaken.

'Incredible!' I said.

'That's the price . . . if you want to give your swallows a home for the summer.'

The expert went away and did not come back. I said to myself that there must surely be a cheaper way of mending the roof. There was no need for a show roof, a professional roof. All that was needed to be done was to replace the ripped away planks and stop the roof from leaking. Then the swallows and their nest would be secure and dry.

'What shall I do?' I asked Jeannie.

'See Bill. He'll give you an idea.'

Bill Trevorrow was a long-time neighbour, always helpful. And I went to see him and he came down and inspected the roof. Instead of talking in terms of a dream roof, he suggested that all I needed was chipboard and a roll or two of felt to nail on the chipboard. It sounded easy.

'What is chipboard?' I asked him, 'and where do I get it?'

This was another stage in my education of working on my own. Matters which practical people thought of as normal, were to me strange. Chipboard?

'Look in *The Cornishman*,' said Bill. 'You'll see advertisements there for cut-price chipboard.'

I looked in *The Cornishman*, our admirable local newspaper, and saw such an advertisement. One morning Jeannie and I drove over to the suppliers near Hayle and bought the chipboard, six large oblongs, the quantity, so Bill advised me, that I would need. Cost £30.

Within a few days, these oblongs were delivered at Minack, each one far heavier than I had expected, each an inch thick, and I learnt they were made of compressed sawdust. But now they were here, what was I to do with them? I had a struggle to shift one of them, let alone lift them into position on the roof.

Once again, Jeannie had a good solution.

'Let's get hold of Ted Clements,' she suggested.

We first met Ted when he came to clean our sitting room carpet with one of those large suction machines which seem to turn old carpets into new. He came with his wife Cassie, who had helped us once during a daffodil season. He was young, stocky, dark, with that evangelical look in his eyes of the very Cornish. They lived a few miles away from Minack amidst wild moorland at the base of Carn Brea, the hill from the top of which on a fine day you can survey the whole of West Cornwall. Ted was a handyman. Ted, if he were free, would fix the roof in time for the swallows. There were, I reckoned, ten days left.

We contacted Ted, and he promised to come and inspect the task at the weekend. He duly arrived, optimistically said it would not be too difficult a job, asked me to obtain two rolls of felt and a pound of roofing nails, and promised to come again on the first fine day. Seven days left.

A low now arrived from the Atlantic, and the rain fell and spattered through the gaping roof, and seeped through the rotten planks, dripping on to the ground. Monday, Tuesday, Wednesday, Thursday, then on Friday we woke up to a clear blue sky. Three days left.

'Ted will be here today,' said Jeannie.

He was not.

Instead, soon after midday, Jeannie came rushing to me.

'I've seen a swallow!'

'Where?'

'It dived into the garage and flew out again in disgust!'

She was laughing.

'Now, Jeannie . . . this is serious.'

'All right, I'll go and ring Ted and see what's happened to him.'

When she came back, she said she had talked to Cassie and Cassie had told her that Ted had sprained his wrist badly, could not lift anything, and had gone to the doctor.

'Disaster,' I said.

'Yes,' agreed Jeannie.

Saturday, Sunday, both fine days.

Then, on Monday, Ted arrived.

'Ted,' I said, 'you can't lift anything.'

'Oh yes I can.'

Then he looked at me without a trace of embarrassment and explained what had happened.

'The doctor,' he said, 'told me not to use my wrist for a week, but last night I went to St Just Free Church, where a healer was holding a service. I am a member of the Church. The healer touched my wrist . . . and all the pain went away.'

He walked over to one of the heavy chipboard oblongs.

'Look,' he said, lifting up one end. 'Easy!'

Just in time. The following morning our pair of swallows swooped into the garage, swooped in and out all day, approved of what had been done, and stayed with us all summer.

TEN

I wonder why I react as I do towards episodes such as the arrival of the swallows. Why should I have felt concern as to whether or not they had a dry roof for their nest? It was such a trivial matter; as trivial as the pleasure I had when Oliver suddenly appeared and joined me in a stroll down the lane, or when I watched Ambrose sitting on the granite rock beside the white seat in front of the barn, resembling a miniature lion as Monty once did; or when I had the fun of watching Fred and Merlin racing around a field. All apparently trivial, yet not trivial to me.

Perhaps my reaction is due to a nostalgia for my youth, for the friends of my youth. Perhaps I am identifying the innocence of animals with the innocence of my friends who were killed in the Hitler war. My friends possessed an innocence which let them believe that it was worth dying for the cause for which they were fighting. Their innocence let them be convinced that the future, a calm, contented future, enjoying the basic values, was in their hands. If the war were won, their sacrifice would not be in vain. I ponder about my young friends who were killed, as I stand in a meadow staring out to sea, or look at a wild violet or a primrose, or hear a robin sing, or am aware of anything that shares the innocence of my friends who were killed. Cynics will smile at my thoughts. Political activists, deaf to a robin's song, blind to a primrose, will stand up on their rostrums. Sacrifice? Risk being killed? Fools that they did not belong to a union which demanded danger money before battle.

Innocence, in these rushing times, is becoming a lost virtue. Innocence is an ally to magic. Innocence does not spoil wonder by analysing it. Innocence is the acceptance of the unexplained. It offers trust and respect, offers pride in work conscientiously carried out. Innocence enables you to believe that miracles are possible. Innocence means good manners. It is without guile, envy or hate. Innocence is a victim of the materialistic society.

May . . . and Minack had become a large, unseen housing estate. Wrens rushed in one direction, blackbirds in another, a feather in a beak or a moustache of dried grass. A woodpecker tapped at his circular hole in a tree, pigeons cooed, a thrush built a nest in the tractor shelter on a Saturday and a Sunday, then glared at me balefully on the Monday as I revved up the tractor engine, deserting the nest on Tuesday. Charlie the chaffinch preened himself on the bird table, shouting 'cheep, cheep', then away across the stable meadow to the undergrowth by the reservoir. Up on the chimney of solid granite, Philip the gull foolishly believed his mate would call it home, bringing tufts of grass, squawking. Bluetits, like flecks of summer sea, flitted in the wood; chiff-chaffs answered one another; Robert the robin begged for home-made bread, filled his beak, watched us warily, waiting for us to go out of sight. And all the while our pair of swallows were joyously flying around the cottage, skimming the donkey field, up around the chimney, black spots against white clouds, twittering, dashing in and out of the garage. May . . . and the Minack unseen housing estate was full.

I now played the role of guardian to this unseen housing estate. I was like a policeman protecting the inhabitants from robbers and violence. I had no fear of sinister intent on the part of Oliver and Ambrose because they, like

Monty and Lama before them, showed no inclination to catch birds. Strange that they did not have a natural cat instinct to do so, though there was always the risk that they might mistake the movement of a bird on the ground for the movement of a mouse. I was not, therefore, concerned about Oliver and Ambrose. My fears centred around the pair of carrion crows who habitually built a nest in Minack wood . . . and the magpies. These were the villains, the ruthless mafia which threatened every nest in the housing estate, feeding off the eggs, feeding off the fledglings. Time and again in the past, I had seen evidence of the destruction they inflicted, and this year I was determined to prevent it.

I was a victim, however, of that kind of liberalism which permits a murderer, a terrorist for instance, to live several years in peace at the taxpayers' expense instead of following the Bible's dictum of 'an eye for an eye; a tooth for a tooth'. I could not, therefore, despite the murderous qualities of the carrion crows and the magpies, shoot them. Nor could I tolerate the prospect of anyone else shooting them. Hence I devised another way of controlling the villains of the unseen housing estate. I did not enjoy carrying out my plan; indeed I hated doing so, but I saw no alternative if the estate were to live in safety.

'It's time I did it,' I said to Jeannie one morning, steeling myself.

'I know how you feel. How many are there?'

'The carrion crows are in the top of one of the ash trees. One magpie nest is in the wood above the spot where the donkeys sometimes shelter, another is among the blackthorn near to the small reservoir, and there is a third in the copse down the cliff.'

'Just think,' Jeannie said, sympathetically, 'how many fledglings would be devoured to feed all that lot. You're doing the right thing, I'm sure of it.'

'Thank you for the encouragement.'

I went out and collected the long aluminium pipe, a relic of an irrigation scheme we once installed, and then I carried it through the orchard, past the hut where

Boris the drake used to sleep at night, and into the area where the tall ash trees grow. High above me was the nest, resembling an upside down guardsman's busby and, as I came under it, a carrion crow flew away.

The success of my plan depended on timing. I had to watch the nest being built, I had to wait until the eggs were laid . . . for my plan, knowing that carrion crows and magpies had only one brood a year, was to destroy the nest after the eggs had been laid. For every egg destroyed, any number of fledglings, adult birds as well, would be saved.

I manoeuvred the long aluminium pipe until it was underneath the nest, and then began pushing the pipe at the sticks, twigs and grass until it began to fall apart, and first one greeny-brown egg crashed to the ground, then another. I then proceeded to the magpie nest in the wood, where the task was repeated; and after that, I went to the magpie nest near the small reservoir. When that had been dealt with, I knew that two young carrion crows and eight young magpies would not any longer be devouring the young inhabitants of the unseen housing estate.

There was only one magpie nest left, in the copse down the cliff, and I thereupon set off with my long aluminium pipe to complete the task I had set myself. I clambered down with difficulty through the thicket until I reached a position directly beneath the beehive-type nest, a position which gave me an easy opportunity to demolish the nest and the eggs it contained. I had the pipe poised in the manner of a javelin thrower when, a split second before I was about to jab at the nest, I suddenly heard from above my head, a soft burbling. I put the pipe aside, then struggled up through the blackthorn surrounding the nest until I could see inside. My timing, my plan to destroy the nest before the young had been hatched, had failed. Four tiny magpies were huddled together, waiting to be fed. I left them there.

Was I right? I do not know. Their appetites required the parents to ravage the unseen estate, that is for certain, and when they left the nest in due course, exotic though they may have looked, they cackled their harsh call and increased the range of their attacks. One casualty I feel sure was theirs. I was standing on the bridge on a Monday morning at the end of June, and Charlie the chaffinch had been with me, shouting at me so persistently that I had said to him: 'Shut your beak!' I had spoken to him many, many times in this way during the six years he had been with us. That morning, I watched him fly back to the undergrowth near the little reservoir, where I guessed he had his young, expecting him to return soon as he usually did. After a few minutes, Jeannie called me and I went indoors but, as we were talking, we both heard a terrible commotion outside and we rushed out to see what it was. Over amongst the undergrowth surrounding the small reservoir was a group of five magpies.

We have never seen Charlie again.

The donkeys, meanwhile, had already played their own part in creating the unseen housing estate. Penny, when she was alive, black-coated Penny, was popular among the jackdaw colony, which inhabited a steep cliff not far away. The black hairs of her coat were considered by these jackdaws to provide high-class furnishing for their nests, and they would descend upon her, two or three at a time, tugging at the hairs until their beaks were full. Fred was not so popular, presumably because they did not fancy the coffee colour of his coat, and he would stand watching the favoured Penny, perplexed.

Fred, at this time of year, also had another problem. He began shedding his winter coat at the end of April; first a tuft or two here and there, then gradually, as the weeks went by, the tufts became large patches, and his coat developed an appearance that suggested he had been attacked by a concourse of moths. In any year this was a period of embarrassment for him, but at least when Penny was alive he was able to share his embarrassment, for she too lost her winter coat during the early summer.

This did not apply to Mingoose Merlin. Mingoose Merlin was resplendent. His long, dark brown coat draped over him as if it were an exotic rug, and hair covering his eyes so that one had to push it back to see them, and each of his sturdy legs looking as if they wore stockings of silky wool. No wonder the jackdaws chose him for their furnishings. No wonder they pecked at his coat with the same frantic zest as customers in a department-store sale.

Poor Fred. A blue summer sky, a soft breeze from the sea, holidays in the air, and someone would call on us and see Merlin, and cry out: 'He's beautiful!' But only take an embarrassed glance towards Fred.

We too felt embarrassed. We had to admit that Fred looked as if he qualified for an entry into a donkey home catering for ill-treated donkeys. He looked bedraggled, and when anyone arrived to see him, I found myself spluttering excuses and trying to manoeuvre him out of sight and weakly permitting the focus to be on Merlin. Not that it needed much effort on my part to have the focus on Merlin. He asked for it; expected it. He came trotting happily towards visitors, pushing his head towards them when he arrived, conveying a mood of a dog-like friendliness . . . while Fred stayed glumly in the background.

Fred was soon to find himself in a particularly embarrassing situation, almost a sad one. We had been visited by a young schoolmaster, who told us that he was in charge of thirty twelve- and thirteen-year-olds from the Midlands who were camping in the area, and that he wondered whether we would allow them to visit the donkeys. Of course, we agreed, and we proceeded to arrange the date and time for the occasion. All was settled, and the teacher, an earnest, conscientious young man had begun to walk up the lane, when he suddenly paused, and came back a few steps.

'I think I ought to tell you something,' he said, very solemnly.

'Oh,' I said, 'what's that?'

'Well,' he replied, shyly, 'I think you ought to know that the children are less able children.'

'Less able?'

'They're not quite . . .'

'I understand,' I said, quickly.

The day, the hour, arrived for the visit and Jeannie and I waited apprehensively.

'We had better stay glued to the donkeys,' said Jeannie. 'If the children are as we're told they are, anything might happen.'

'Would you like to hold Merlin's halter, or Fred's?'

'I think I'll hold Merlin,' Jeannie replied.

We went down to the stable meadow, fixed the halters, and soon after we heard a murmur of voices from the direction of the cliff path, then through the much-nibbled white gate which divides us from the cliff appeared a troop of laughing, excited children. They hurried up the path, shouted cries of delight when they saw the donkeys and, forthwith, surrounded them. The young teacher and his colleague followed in the rear, reached a pleasant patch of grass, undid the satchels from their backs, sat down and, I felt, were thankful for a short rest from looking after their charges.

Jeannie and I and the donkeys were now alone with the children. Chatter, excitement, the innocent wish for enjoyment, and soon there was that inevitable cry: 'Can I have a ride? Can I?'.

It was a nostalgic cry for Jeannie and me. It was a cry we first heard when Fred had his first birthday party, when he was king of the afternoon, surrounded by guests who offered to share with him their ice-creams, young guests from St Buryan school, who clustered round him as he was led up to see the birthday cake specially made for him, with a single candle upon it, which he blew out theatrically, by pushing his nostrils at it, to the applause of everyone present, including a boy who had come to the party dressed up as the Mad Hatter.

It was different on this occasion. Merlin was the centre of attention. Moth-eaten Fred, bedraggled Fred, received passing references, but it was Merlin who, this time, was the king. 'Can I have a ride? Can I?' And when I listened to these calls, the years slipped away, and I thought of my philosophy that time should never be measured in years; that time should never be considered as a number of yearly hills to be reached, calendar stepping-stones to retirement pension and death . . . but that time should be viewed as if it were a plain. Ask most people . . . some moment, some incident, some emotion, will return, awoken by a flash of connection, and be as purely vivid as when it first happened. As I heard the children calling for a ride on Merlin, I heard the voices calling for a ride on Fred.

It was Merlin's afternoon; it was particularly Merlin's afternoon because he had never given rides before, and he loved doing so. Jeannie had no trouble leading him around, and the children queued up and behaved with perfect manners, and filled the stable meadow with fun and naturalness and innocence.

'Less able?' I said to Jeannie, after it was all over. 'Tell me, what does it mean? The children were as bright as buttons.'

'Apparently,' said Jeannie, 'teachers have to fill in a form placing each child under their care in one of five categories. "Less able" is one of the categories, and all it means is that they are not considered to be up to the normal standard for reading and writing.'

'What a stupid phrase to use. I would have had an inferiority complex for life if I had been labelled "less able".'

'You were,' said Jeannie, laughing.

'Now I come to think of it, you're quite right. I didn't pass any exams, and when I dropped a catch in a crucial inter-house cricket match there was that remark by my indignant housemaster: "You're useless to society, Tangye".'

'There you are,' said Jeannie, 'and I'm sure you were as bright as a button too!'

'Scares me the way sensitive children can be hurt by the remarks of adults.'

'And sensitive donkeys!'

Fred, however, on that day the children came, had reached the lowest level of his bedraggled appearance and soon there were signs that his new coat had begun to grow and he began to be jaunty again. Instead of hiding from visitors, he too began coming to the gate. A sheen soon glowed on his coat and, instead of being ignored, there were cries of admiration and cameras clicked and there was a look in Fred's eye which seemed to say: 'I am the king again!' The reason for his confidence was easy to understand, for while he blossomed, Merlin was becoming threadbare. Merlin's time to lose his coat had arrived. In Fred's case, one had felt sad; in Merlin's, it was funny. The loss of his coat made him appear as if he were covered by layer upon layer of fringes; the tassel-like fringes of an old Victorian tablecloth. Fred's coat being short had moulted away without aid, but with Merlin it was different. His long coat had to be helped, and this was done by vigorous brushing.

One day, while I was doing this, a little girl called Tracey visited us and she proceeded to help, brushing Merlin with such success that she soon had two large handfuls of his hair. Her mother asked whether they could take it away with them. We heard nothing from them for several months, but then a parcel arrived, and in the parcel was a ball of Merlin's hair woven into a yarn like knitting wool . . . and a tea cosy with the outline of two donkeys stitched with Merlin's yarn. Thus, with Merlin's help, our morning tea is kept warm. Merlin, although he looked funny as he lost his coat, was useful.

It was during this period that an incident occurred which made me look very foolish. I had spent ten minutes one evening brushing Merlin and, when I had finished, I stayed on with him, teasing him with the mouthpiece of my pipe. I felt he needed attention and so I played with him, absentmindedly, poking his nose with the pipe as I stood by the small gate above the cottage at the entrance to the donkey field. I have no idea what I was thinking about, my thoughts were far away, when suddenly I saw the mouthpiece of my pipe disappearing inside Merlin's mouth while I was left holding the bowl.

I panicked. I had been warned time and again that the throat of a donkey can be easily choked (donkeys must never be given meat) because it is narrow, and I immediately imagined, because it was evening and I was tired, that there would be unpleasant complications.

I ran back to the cottage to find Jeannie.

'Merlin has swallowed the mouthpiece of my pipe!' I cried out.

'How could he possibly have done that?'

'Never mind how he has swallowed it . . . he just did. So what shall I do?'

Jeannie was as worried as I was.

'Go and ring the vet,' she said quickly.

I jumped into the car and speeded towards the village of Sheffield, where stands our nearest call-box and, once there, 2p in my hand, I dialled the vet. Buzz, buzz, a man answered but, alas, the vet on duty was not the vet I knew. The vet I knew was aware of our eccentricities, our animal hypochondria, and I would have felt at ease if, as I stood in the call-box, I had told him Merlin had consumed the mouthpiece of my pipe. But the vet on duty was a stranger.

'I was poking the donkey with my pipe,' I explained, with some embarrassment, 'then the mouthpiece suddenly disappeared. The donkey must have grabbed it.'

'Oh, yes,' said the vet on duty, politely.

'I'm so sorry to trouble you, but I'm just ringing up to see if I should do anything urgent about it.'

There was a pause. Then came the brisk answer.

'No cause to worry,' the vet said, 'and if you want to retrieve the mouthpiece of your pipe, wait twenty-four hours, then walk round the field where you left the donkey. You'll find the mouthpiece where he has been standing.'

I never did find it.

By now, our three hundred Maascross tomato plants had reached their fruiting time and people were especially asking for them, saying that they tasted like the tomatoes they used to know long ago. The two greenhouses in which they were planted with plenty of space between each plant, so giving light and air, were not show greenhouses. By that I mean they were not neat and tidy as I would have liked. It was just that Jeannie and I did not have the time to keep them so. There were weeds like fat-hen and, on the sides, there was a sinister encroachment of couch grass. But we did not worry unduly. We were on our own and we could not cope with every problem that faced us. We had to shut our eyes, check ourselves from being over-conscientious, and so enjoy the freedom of waking up in the morning and being responsible to no one, not even to an employee.

The Orlyt greenhouse, the one-hundred feet by twenty-feet Orlyt in front of the cottage, had become a greenhouse of experiments. We had grown the previous winter and into the early spring conventional crops like a succession of lettuce and Early Onward peas, and they had given us a satisfactory reward. We felt, however, that we wanted to find a crop that would thrive in a greenhouse, but which would not take the labour time and cost of the tomato crop.

The previous summer I used to see from time to time a famous grower and friend of long standing called Leslie Noye bringing runner beans into Penzance for sale. His were open-grown runner beans, and it occurred to me that I could beat him to the market with the first runner beans if we grew them in one of our greenhouses. I was warned by horticultural experts that it would be impossible. Runner beans would not pollinate under glass so early in the year because there were no bees to help them. Jeannie had the answer.

'Those sweet peas in the Orlyt we had last year,' she said, 'they brought in the bees. They'll do it again.'

And this is what happened. Our Knee-Hi sweet peas in the Orlyt began blooming in the very early summer (and continued to do so until September) and they brought in the bees and so the runner beans were pollinated.

'Leslie,' I said, one late June morning when I saw him in Penzance, 'I'm selling runner beans!'

'You *are*?' he replied in an incredulous voice.

One of the amusements of a grower is bantering another.

We also grew cucumbers in the Orlyt, and melons, and we had a patch of Cape Gooseberry plants where Jeannie, in previous times, had her geraniums. Jeannie's geraniums had become a menace. She kept on taking cuttings, sticking them into the Orlyt where they proliferated, became elongated, and although colourful to look at, were only taking up useful space. I had to persuade her gently to let me remove them, for she had an affection for her geraniums out of proportion to their value. There was another reason for her concern for the geraniums. Frogs. Frogs lived among the geraniums, but removing the geraniums did not remove the frogs. They moved elsewhere in the Orlyt, among the sweet peas, among the runner beans, among the Cape Gooseberries. There were big frogs, medium-sized frogs, and little frogs not much bigger than a thumbnail. I would wonder whether they felt imprisoned in the Orlyt; pleasant enough for them in winter, but a hot desert in the summer except under the foliage, so when I found a frog I would carefully pick it up and carry it quickly to the undergrowth by the little stream outside the far end of the Orlyt and it would hop away within it.

I had to be careful, too, when I picked the cucumbers in case I trod on one hiding among the sprawling leaves, for I did not train the cucumbers upwards on wires as normally is done, but let them spread over the ground. Nor did I engage in the professional task of pinching out the laterals, though my laziness did not seem to affect the quality and the quantity of the crop. In July and August I was picking fat, juicy cucumbers, far too many for salad use, and Jeannie would turn them into soup. When I carried yet another armful to her, she would cry: 'Not another lot!' Jeannie was a queen of cucumber soup. In August and September she spent much time making it, and it is so delicious a soup that I must give here the recipe. Once prepared, she puts it in cartons in the freezer and, during the months ahead, a carton will be brought out and the contents served cold in the manner of *Vichyssoise*. The recipe comes from the American magazine *Gourmet*, for which Jeannie writes.

2 large cucumbers; 2 oz butter; 1 onion; 1 pint milk; ¼ pint double cream; salt and pepper; 2 tablespoons flour.

Peel cucumbers, dice into small pieces, put them in a large pan in the melted butter, cook slowly until soft and mushy. Peel onion, put it into a pan with a pint of milk, salt and pepper, and simmer. Stir two table-spoons of flour into the cucumber mixture and cook slowly, stirring most of the time, until the flour is dissolved and cooked. Now strain the milk over this mixture and bring to the boil. Remove pan from heat and strain into a bowl. Put strained soup back in pan and add the cream, bring just to the boil and cook gently, stirring. Taste for seasoning, you may need more salt. Now strain through a nylon sieve into a bowl and leave to cool. When left in the freezer, take the carton out the night before using, when it is advisable to strain again into soup tureen.

At intervals during our activity, Oliver and Ambrose enjoyed the quiet of the Orlyt. Oliver and Ambrose deeply loved each other. Ambrose, after some adventurous excursion in the area, after an absence of three or four hours, would return, see Oliver and run to him, as if he were glad to be able to tell him the story of the particular adventure. Oliver, however, still maintained the discipline that he had imposed on Ambrose from the moment he brought him into our lives. He bashed Ambrose with a paw if he thought he was too excited; bashed him during the night when both were on our bed and Ambrose, for no special reason, was purring full throttle. Such loud purrs kept Oliver awake, and he objected to them.

But they enjoyed their quiet times in the Orlyt among the cucumbers and the melons and the runner beans, the sweet peas and the Cape Gooseberries and the frogs. A blackbird or two would also be hopping around and, occasionally, Robert the robin who, when he was young, we used to watch being fed by Charlie the chaffinch. I wonder whether it often happens that a chaffinch pops food into a baby robin's beak.

Their quiet times were spent in the bracken I stored in the Orlyt for the donkeys' winter bedding or, more popular still, on a discarded bolster where they huddled close together, black and orange side by side. This bolster lay against a bag of potting compost, and it is evidence of what happens when a one-time cat hater becomes cat addicted that I never dared use the compost while they slept on the bolster. I did not want to experience the lifting of the head, the glare, the whole ambience of disapproval that would be inflicted upon me. 'You're a nut case,' said a non-F friend, when I told him this.

It was on cool summer days that they used the Orlyt, when the rains fell and the winds blew, and when it was hot they had their hiding places in the bracken on the way up to the well, or in the mass of grass above the white seat, or in spots we never could find. Or they would lie on the garage roof, two inches of roofing felt and chipboard between them and the second brood of swallows, no sign of concern on the part of the parents, no interest shown in them by Oliver and Ambrose.

Up on our own roof, along the apex of the roof, would perch Ron the rook and, during the course of the summer, he had brought, from time to time, his mate whom we called Eth; then later they arrived with two young rooks. All four would patiently wait for bread to be thrown to them; and as they waited, Ron and Eth would make strange noises, not the customary caw-caw, but a gurgle like the sound of water running down a waste-pipe. Ron was always the first to reach the bread and, since he was the resident rook, it was natural that he should do so. He looked funny sometimes. If we misfired when throwing up the bread and it landed low down the roof near the gutter, Ron, from his perch on the apex of the roof, would slide to it on his bottom, black wings flapping, as if he were on a toboggan. Having had their fill, all four would fly away, over the greenhouses in the direction of Lamorna woods.

It was not easy for Ron, however, to collect his share of the bread when Philip the gull was there. Philip considered the roof was his territory and, when he came sailing up from the cliffs and found Ron already in position, he would squawk, charge at him with beating wings and attempt to drive him away. Ron was too cunning to meet Philip face to face, and he would retreat to the far end of the roof, or make a token flight round the donkey field, then return. When bread was thrown on the roof, however, he was always the loser. Philip was too strong for Ron.

The winds came early that autumn and Ron stayed away from the roof. Philip, unafraid of the wind, would circle above us, hover for a moment like a hawk, then float down to the roof, wings spread out, a balancing act that was beautiful to watch. The swallows had left. The donkeys, vexed by the wind, would stand with bottoms to a hedge. Oliver and Ambrose would curl close together on the bolster in the Orlyt.

Above them, leaves fell on the glass like confetti.

ELEVEN

The winter in Cornwall is more soothing than summer. In summer one sometimes senses a mood of anxiety . . . holidaymakers worry about the weather, shopkeepers whether they will dispose of the stocks they hold, hoteliers about their bookings. The holiday trade rules the summer and gives it a touch of restlessness. Permanent inhabitants need its success to provide them with their income, holidaymakers deserve value for their money. Everyone, in their different roles, striving hard to make it successful, and so much depends on the weather. The sun is hot and Jeannie says to me: 'I'm so glad for the holidaymakers.' The postman arrives, a seaman's oiler buttoned up to his neck, the rain drenching him as he hands us the letters at the porch door:

'Terrible for the holidaymakers, terrible.'

A special charm of Cornwall is the concern that local people have for holidaymakers. Their concern is nothing to do with their need to earn a living. It is a natural wish for visitors to be happy. This wish is expressed in simple ways like the way porters at Penzance Station greet arrivals, and the way those in small shops treat customers in the manner of old-fashioned village shops. Customers may obtain 2p off a tin of beans in a supermarket, but they have to queue to pay and they have lost the intangible pleasure of personal service in a small shop. It is the same with places to stay. Go to a computer-controlled hotel, one of a chain, and there is a remorseless feeling that you are a holidaymaker on a conveyor belt. In on a Saturday, out on a Saturday, a unit on a computer.

But come to some places I know, and you will receive the effortless welcome, the genuine wish to please, that would not fit into any computer programme since it has nothing to do with figures or logic. Come, for instance, to Nancy Warne, whose guesthouse is opposite the Lamorna Post Office; or Mary Clements near Lamorna Bridge, who will send her guests, if they wish, fresh violets in the winter, picked from meadows close to where they have stayed; or Mrs Jeffreys of the old farmhouse of Tregurno, where we used to stay before moving into Minack, and who is a gourmet cook; or Linda Prowse in the beautifully kept farmhouse halfway up Boleigh Hill on the right; or the camp site of the Eddys next door; or the farm of Roselucumbe, where Linda's son Owen, and Theresa, his wife, treat guests as if they belonged to the family . . . all these will give you a welcome which will be an echo of the holiday you dreamt about when you were a child.

Unfortunately, there are those who exploit this goodwill of the Cornish, who commercialise the romance of Cornwall and who bring attitudes of behaviour along with them which are more in tune with city life. Council-planning authorities watch the situation imaginatively, but it is not easy for them to condemn commercial development in view of Cornwall's economic situation. The true Cornwall may be a haven of naturalness and a quiet way of living, but this does not help to find jobs. The job situation is the conundrum of Cornwall. Unemployment is not a passing phase; it is here for ever because Cornwall is too far away from the centre of industrial activity to attract large industrial firms. Many of us may be thankful that this is so, but it is a bleak prospect for the youth of Cornwall. It is no comfort to them to be told that a Midlands-type industrialisation of Cornwall would take away the gentle way of living they now can enjoy.

Hence commercialisation of the romance of Cornwall is one way of denting unemployment, but it has its dangers. A cove, for instance, much loved over the years by the few, will be envisaged by some entrepreneur as an opportunity to benefit the many, and a functional café will be built and a barrack-type public convenience and an asphalt-covered car park. Employment will have been given, but the magic of the cove lost and another part of the romance of Cornwall chipped away. A cove I know, a lovely, lonely cove with a pocket of sandy beach, had, to local amusement, its revenge on this kind of vandalism. True, there was no café, no public convenience, but a large car park was built in its vicinity so that people in their dozens could enjoy its hitherto secret seclusion. The car park was built in time to capture the arrival of the summer season . . . but there was no sandy beach to enjoy. Storms during the winter had filled it with boulders.

There is another form of commercialisation which one may be suspicious of, may dislike, but which brings a form of employment to Cornwall. This is the acquisition of cottages as holiday homes by people who live on the other side of the Tamar. People who buy such holiday homes usually have neat, urban ideas of how their holiday homes should be, and so money is spent on them and employment given to dress up the old cottages and houses to the same standard of appearance as the homes the new owners live in for the majority of the year.

You pass these cottages and, for most of the year, the curtains are drawn. Yet, although no pulse is beating in these homes, no life from them entering into the neighbouring community, it remains a fact that useful employment has been temporarily given to those who performed the decoration. Sadly, this benefit is countered by its effect on the locals who are looking for permanent homes. Prices are now far, far out of reach of their pockets.

Winter, and reality returns to Cornwall; reality in the form of lonely beaches, rain-bashed moorland bracken exposing summer-hidden rocks, flotsam of foam floating up from the cliffs. The ebbing and surging of wind

147

through the trees; no walkers tramping the coastal path. The *Scillonian* plunging on the way to the islands. Bluetits, after their summer absence, dancing around the bird table; a pair of fieldfares from over the Channel making sudden dashes across the stable meadow grass; a wren searching for a cold weather hiding place. Buds on the white camellia bush; a last rose above the grave where Lama lies. Muddy boots, a log fire, isolation and always the winds, the winds.

'Two panes gone in the Orlyt,' I said to Jeannie.

'Now, be careful.'

'Have done them already.'

'That's clever of you, but I worry.'

'Me too, but not the way you do. I'm worrying about the condition of the whole greenhouse. I can cope with the odd pane, but the frames are showing signs of rot in some places and some of the lathes holding the glass are warped. I don't like the look of it.'

'And the winter just begun.'

'Yes.'

There is fun about preparing for winter, about behaving with the foresight of squirrels, stocking up with fruits and vegetables and being thankful for the invention of the freezer. Peas are the base of our frozen vegetables and blackberries for fruit. Nothing original about either, but they are easy to store, easy to gather and, although many other items go into the two freezers we have, peas and blackberries provide the out-of-season foundation.

Blackberries easy to gather, did I say? This autumn had been the first blackberry time that Mingoose Merlin had been with us. We had had, of course, experience of the way that Penny and Fred behaved in their liking for blackberries, but they never had a passion for them. Merlin had such a passion. Normally we went black-berrying in places that were inaccessible for donkeys, like down the cliff where there were particularly luscious blackberries. There we were safe to gather them. But when we took Fred and Merlin for a walk, blackberries to be gathered on the way, we learnt by experience that we had to be very smart to gather them before Merlin devoured them.

It was on one of these expeditions that Merlin at last jumped the stream that crossed the path on the way to Lamorna, the stream which Fred had also refused to jump when he had been Merlin's age, and we celebrated the occasion by walking on along the badger-like track through the bracken to the tarmac lane which leads down to Lamorna village and The Wink. Merlin's first visit to our outer world. Merlin with ears pricked, me holding fast to the halter, scared he might suddenly take fright and try to dash away.

A quite unnecessary worry. Fred, as an old hand of such visits, displayed a sedate manner of behaviour, showed Merlin that by behaving well there were rewards to be had. On this occasion the landlords, Bob and Di Drennen, and Ann their helper and special friend, whose father Tom used to keep The Wink, produced potato crisps as a reward. Then Di telephoned the Lamorna Post Office where lived, at that time, Mrs Murley, a long-time lover of donkeys, especially of Penny and Fred to whom she thrust carrots whenever we brought them to see her. Mrs Murley was round at The Wink within minutes of the 'phone call, a cluster of carrots in her hand. Mingoose Merlin became over-excited by such generosity and I had to cling to his halter. Fred, however, was dignified. Fred knew that generosity deserved good manners in return. Fred gave Mrs Murley, the post-mistress, a donkey ride.

We had given up wine-making. We had given up trying to coax elderberry flowers into champagne, their berries into red wine. We were failures at wine-making and it was best to admit it. The champagne was always flat and the red wine horrid. I know the reason. Always, during the process of making it, we lost interest, or we were too occupied in doing something else and thus the wine did not receive the cosseting it required. On the other hand, we became expert makers of sloe gin, and sloe gin joined our winter hoard of blackberries and peas.

The picking of the sloes had similar hazards to the picking of the blackberries, because the blackberry brambles were often intertwined with the blackthorn bushes. So we'd each carried two bags: one for blackberries, one for the sloes. This dual picking required concentration, or else a blackberry would go into a sloe bag, or a sloe into a blackberry bag. Merlin did not help. Merlin scorned sloes but, as I reached into a thicket to pick some, pushing my hand through the needle-sharp branches, Merlin would make a grab at a cluster of blackberries that my plunge into the thicket had brought to light.

Sloe gin is much less trouble to make than wine, and we discovered its secret when a gentleman called on us one day. A modest, mild gentleman, who confided to us that he had achieved little in life to be proud of, except for one aspect. He was a successful maker of sloe gin.

'I've brought you a bottle of my vintage,' he said, hesitantly, 'and I would like to give you the secret of my recipe.'

Naturally we greeted this unusual gesture with gratitude. Our gratitude persists. And here is the secret recipe:

Four pounds of sloes to two pounds of sugar and two bottles of gin. You put the sloes into a wine jar, followed by the sugar and the gin, and within three months, after straining, it is ready to drink. Wait longer, and it will mature with increasing depth of flavour and, in any case, you will have three bottles of liqueur which would cost £7 a bottle in the shops.

However, I must tell you our gentleman friend's secret, which placed his sloe gin into a class of its own. You do not just drop each sloe into the wine jar . . . you first snip them with a pair of scissors. The scissors are the secret. They cut the skin, loosen the juice, and the consequence is a liqueur that, accompanied by Jeannie's coconut cake, is my particular gourmet delight.

The scissor part of the exercise did, however, require patience. We sat opposite sides of the table in the porch, wine jar in front of us, sloes in front of us, scissors in our hands and proceeded to snip, snip, snip. My arm would become stiff, my fingers sticky with the juice and, uncharitably, I would say: 'I hope we are going to keep it all to ourselves.' Such a selfish thought, I knew, would never materialise into reality. Jeannie is an instant giver. Jeannie has no inhibitions about giving. Jeannie's aim is to make people happy—even at my snipping expense.

We sat there snipping one afternoon and suddenly heard an explosion of a green woodpecker's call. Normally you can describe the call as a form of laughter. There is no urgency about it, a noisy chuckle perhaps . . . but, when there is a sudden explosion of its call, one knows that it is being attacked. Its slow up-and-down flight is menacingly vulnerable.

Jeannie dropped scissors, dropped sloes and was out through the porch door and away. I soon followed her but, by the time I reached her, she had run down the path, turned left, and was kneeling on the grass near the rose garden. As I arrived, I heard the flutter of wings and then saw the woodpecker take off, making a noise as if it were

151

hysterically laughing, its bouncing flight taking it to the safety of the wood.

'My goodness,' said Jeannie, 'that was a near thing.'

'The sparrow hawk?'

'Yes, it was actually on the woodpecker, pinning it down on the grass! Didn't even see me until I clapped my hands.'

'Marvellous how quick you were.'

'Poor woodpecker.'

'The second you've saved. Two years ago you saved one in the orchard.'

'Same thing happened. I call woodpeckers the cart-horses of the air.'

'That's a funny phrase.'

'Well, they lollop along on regular routes. There's no manoeuvrability about them like other birds. I've seen that sparrow hawk these past few days on watch on the hawthorn down the path to Fred's field. It stayed there motionless . . . then the woodpecker comes up from the cliff on the way to the wood and that's when the sparrow hawk struck.'

'A very frustrated sparrow hawk at the moment, I feel.'

Jeannie laughed.

'I'm glad to think so.'

Then we returned to our snipping.

My own particular tasks of late autumn, early winter, involved the heavy work, the cutting of the grass and weed growth on the flat daffodil meadows by charging across them with the massive Condor rotary cutter, the clearing of extinct summer crops from the greenhouses, and having a strange satisfaction in slicing away the bracken from the cliff meadows by means of the Japanese brush cutter slung across my shoulders. Satisfaction . . . because no other daffodil meadows on the cliff were now being cared for.

'Why do we do it?' I asked Jeannie. 'Why do we keep these meadows open when an accountant would surely say it was not financially worthwhile?'

'Pride,' said Jeannie. 'You know it's pride. There was

that magical day, before we had even moved in, that we started opening up that meadow right down the bottom of the cliff and we slashed at the undergrowth together and, when the nettles and the brush and the bracken lay flat in front of us, we both had a feeling that a new life had begun for us. True, isn't it?'

'True.'

'Pride in our work. We are lucky . . . the clearing of those tiny meadows, pointless from a money point of view, gives us this pride. If everyone in factories or in any other kind of job, could take a pride in their work, there wouldn't be so many strikes.'

'Boredom, lack of involvement, that helps to breed strikes.'

'I wonder,' said Jeannie, 'how your grandfather would have seen today's industrial situation.'

'Interesting point,' I said. 'I'll look up *One and All* and see if there are clues in it.'

A remarkable man, my grandfather, and I first wrote about him in my book *A Gull on the Roof*. He and his four brothers were born in Illogan near Redruth, their father and mother keeping the village shop and tending a small farm. They were strong-minded, careful parents ('make straight paths to thyself' were the dying words of his mother to Sir Richard, my grandfather); and she, in particular, urged her sons to develop their dawning gifts as engineers. They were very poor and the obstacles to their progress seemed insurmountable. But the time was to come when their name as engineering inventors was known all over the world and their factory in Birmingham employed over two thousand people (unhappily, as in the history of so many family firms, Tangyes faded into obscurity during the third generation).

One and All is my grandfather's autobiography and it displays the extraordinary breadth of interests which he developed during his life; world traveller, an authority on Cromwell, a renowned collector of Wedgwood, philanthropist, and a man in the forefront of liberalising industrial working conditions.

And so, as a result of Jeannie's question, I re-read his book, and another, *Tales of a Grandfather*, and I now quote examples of his character and outlook. He is writing of times at the beginning of the century:

'I believe that most of our men are members of Trades Unions; but during thirty years' experience I only remember one or two instances of interference on their part which I deemed mischievous: while on the other hand, they have many a time rendered considerable assistance by their wise counsels, and it would be disastrous for employers and employed if Trades Unions ceased to exist.'

* * *

'The opposition to the Free Library in Birmingham was composed of very ill-assorted elements; it consisted of the "economists" who opposed any increase of rates for any object; of the publicans, who foresaw that they were not likely to gain by the opening of free libraries; of the extreme Nonconformists, who objected to all rates for such purposes; and of the Clergy, who raised the "religious difficulty" as to books for the people.'

* * *

'I have often heard it said that there are not so many chances for a young man to rise, now-a-days, as formerly. I do not agree with this view. I believe that there are even greater chances for young men than ever before. But these greater opportunities demand greater qualities—qualities that can only be acquired by an increased devotion to study—to greater self-discipline, and to an unconquerable determination to master the principles that underlie the profession or business engaged in. Less opportunity for getting on! Why one of the greatest difficulties of large employers is to find thoroughly capable men to manage the various departments of their concerns; there are many who think themselves capable, but few can stand the test.'

My grandfather, in his later years during a visit to Penzance and Newlyn, had an experience with the staff of Penzance Railway Station which foreshadowed the friendship I have had with members of the staff over the years. A curious story. My grandfather, a teetotaller, wanted one of the famed Newlyn fish dinners and so, surprisingly, he led his party into the Red Lion public house overlooking the harbour. The old lady who was the innkeeper was in a bad mood, told my grandfather that he should not expect fish when the weather was bad, and instead provided him with an undercooked steak, for which he tendered a sovereign and, in return, he received a half sovereign change.

My grandfather's appetite does not seem to have been satisfied by the steak and, later in the afternoon, he went into an hotel near Penzance Station, presumably the Railway Hotel, where he had a more satisfying meal which included apple pie and Cornish cream. At the end of it, he called the waiter, congratulated him on the meal and handed him the half sovereign, the only money he now had with him, which he had received from the old lady of the Red Lion at Newlyn.

The waiter held the half sovereign in his hand for a moment, scrutinising it, then threw it back at Sir Richard and, using the slang of the time, declared angrily: 'It's a rip!' My grandfather thereupon asked to see the landlord and told this gentleman that if he would accompany him across the road to Penzance Station he, Sir Richard, would soon prove his identity. My grandfather, at the time, had foreseen the future publicity value of advertisement hoardings on the railway track and at stations and Tangyes was so advertised that every station master in the country knew the identity of Sir Richard.

So it was at Penzance. At this station, where daily during the season I bring our daffodils, my grandfather and the landlord of the hotel met the station master of the time . . . and the station master, on being told of my grandfather's embarrassment, drew a handful of silver from his pocket and asked my grandfather to take what he required. Kindness of the same nature has been given to me, and Penzance Station has given me friends I will always remember.

There are days during the winter which the Cornish describe as a day lent. It is a day that, during a period of stormy weather, is serene. A day like a summer day, soft, a haze on the sea, a day that causes the birds to break their silence and sing, a day that makes you forget the yesterday of rain clouds billowing in from the south, the shape of upturned mushrooms, forget the rush of the wind through the trees. Such a day was a Sunday in late January and, in the morning of that day, I went for a walk to the Merlin cliff, the cliff meadows where Merlin first saw the *Scillonian*. I had walked quite a distance along the path when I heard a miaow behind me, and it was Oliver. I stopped and he came to me and rubbed his head against my leg and I had a special welling of love for him.

'Oliver,' I said, 'how people would laugh at me for loving a cat as I do you.'

He and Ambrose had a bountiful Christmas; presents had been sent to them, catmint-filled mice, a tin of salmon and a postal-order to pay for two whiting. Fred and Merlin also received a share of presents, including chocolate digestive biscuits, carrots wrapped in Christmas paper and a packet of peppermints. Our own contribution, Jeannie's contribution, of homemade mince pies, unfortunately received the same treatment as those the previous Christmas Eve, Merlin's first at Minack. Jeannie, once again, took the trouble to bake the mince pies, having first made her own special mince-pie mixture, and we waited until near midnight, then called the donkeys to the stables. They remained obstinately at the far end of the stable field. We called them a half dozen times and they would not move. At last we walked across the field, Jeannie carrying her mince pies on a plate and we greeted them gaily, as party-givers treat their guests. Jeannie then held out a mince pie to Merlin. Merlin, as at his first Christmas at Minack, took it from her then spat it out.

'Merlin!' said Jeannie, shocked, 'why can't you be like Fred?'

Fred was glad Merlin was not like him. Fred, on this Christmas Eve, with a roof of stars instead of the stable roof, had the mince pies to himself.

A day lent . . . and Oliver and I took the track down the Merlin cliff, each meadow resembling a giant stepping-stone, each meadow showing the green spires of the daffodils that, within a month, should be in bloom, until I reached the blue elvan rock, partly covered by ivy, half-way down the track. There, because the day was warm and I felt idle, and there are times in life that you are able to smother inhibitions and enjoy pleasure without suffering a sense of guilt, I sat down. I sat down on the rock and, within a few seconds, Oliver had jumped on my lap; an uncomfortable lap because I was sitting at an angle. He gave a miniature yap, looked at me, then began to purr. I sat there, gulls gently gliding in the sky, the Bucks below us. The rock on which I was sitting had witnessed over the centuries some terrifying wrecks on the Bucks.

The Bucks are two rocks that reach up like two fists within shouting distance from the Merlin cliff. At low tide, one can see them clearly but, at high tide, they are just beneath the surface.

There has been no major wreck on the Bucks this century, but a hundred years ago there was a series of tragedies . . . the *Francis and Mary* with coal from Cardiff to Penzance, the *Good Intent* from Par to Newport with iron ore, the *Manitoba*, the *Luigina Reanchette* of Genoa from Montevideo to Antwerp; all four being lost in a period of three years. Most dramatic of the ship-wrecks, however, concerned the *Oriental* and the *Garonne*. The *Oriental* was a barque carrying timber from Quebec to Liverpool, and she turned upside down after striking the Bucks and all her crew were lost. But she still floated, bottom-up, and she was towed into Lamorna Cove and her cargo provided a bonanza for the locals. There is today a house in Lamorna Valley called Oriental Cottage, so called because she was built with timber from the wreck.

A year later, in May 1868, came the tragedy of the *Garonne*, an iron screw-steamer of five-hundred tons, bound for Liverpool from Bordeaux, with a general cargo and a number of passengers on board, including women and children. She hit the innermost rock of the Bucks in thick fog and began immediately to sink, a strong south-westerly driving waves over the deck so that the passengers were unable to reach the boats, and one by one they were swept overboard. Only a little boy out of the seventeen passengers miraculously survived.

Jeannie once played a part in a wreck, a wreck rescue. A French trawler, the *Jeanne Gougy* of Dieppe sailed into the cliffs close to Land's End and, on hearing this on the early morning news, we decided to go over there and have a look.

In my frame of mind of today I would not have done so. I now find the sight of a wreck a distressing experience and that those who gather to stare as the vessel sways doom-ridden against the cliffs and to listen to the ghoulish sound of clanking metal, belong to the same category as those who morbidly enjoy a road accident. But I had to learn. The experience of the *Jeanne Gougy* helped me to learn; so too did that of the *Juan Ferrer*, which foundered at Boscawen Point a couple of miles away from us one foggy night when the nearby coastguard station was unlucky enough not to observe the Spanish ship's approach towards the cliffs. That particular night, we had left Penny and Fred to be free in the Minack cliff meadows and they will have heard the cries of the Spanish seamen as, clinging to salvage wood from the wreck, they drifted with the current past the Bucks, past our meadows. Eleven sailors were drowned. Yet, next day, I was among the ghoulish crowds on the slopes above Boscawen Point, vacuously watching the upturned metal of the *Juan Ferrer* clanking uselessly against the rocks.

Jeannie, however, did not behave uselessly at the death of the *Jeanne Gougy*. There we were watching, watching the coastguards in their brave work, marvelling at the flight of the RAF helicopter hovering feet distant from the cliff, when at last both coastguards and helicopter decided that no more could be done to rescue the crew. Up to that time, twelve of the eighteen crew had been drowned.

It was shortly before noon and Jeannie and I, fascinated like rabbits in headlights, continued to stare at the heaving trawler, deck and wheelhouse clearly visible, only her hull ripped by the rocks. We stood there as the coastguards gathered up the lifesaving equipment, as the Sennen Lifeboat sailed away, as the helicopter rose up towards Culdrose aerodrome . . . moment of finality.

Then Jeannie saw the movement of a hand behind the glass that fronted the wheelhouse . . . someone beside her saw it too and they both called out:

'There's a man alive down there!'

The helicopter was recalled, the coastguards returned with their equipment and there followed one of the most remarkable rescue achievements of the Cornish coast. The *Jeanne Gougy* was now on her side and the waves of the ground swell breaking over her, when a man appeared at the side of the wheelhouse. The coastguards fired a line and the man grasped it, managed to secure it, and was hauled to safety in the breeches buoy. Then three men appeared on the fo'c's'le and they too were hauled to safety. No sign of anyone else . . . but the helicopter was now hovering and a crew member was lowered and we watched with trepidation as he disappeared from view *inside* the wheelhouse. An anguished two minutes, then he was in sight again and we watched him being winched up to the helicopter, holding a man in the safety harness. A few minutes later, he was down in the wheelhouse again, then up with another man. I marvel at the bravery of the helicopter crews who patrol the Cornish coast.

A day lent . . . I sat there on the blue elvan rock with Oliver purring on my lap, my mind far, far away from wrecks and stormy seas. There was no logical sequence in my thoughts. I was in one of those rare, hazy moods when the mind is unaffected by immediate problems and you find yourself roaming over a multitude of haphazard ideas which come welling up from the subconscious . . . compassion, which is free, is becoming a rare gift . . . one looks back, cursing oneself for one's mistakes, but forgetful of the climate in which the mistakes were made . . . the generation gap is created by parents . . . one throws a tennis ball (of friendship, of conversation, of an idea) and the receiver muffs the return . . . my generation is kept perpetually young by the media's obsession with the Hitler war . . . sensitive people can understand the philistines, but the philistines will never understand the sensitive . . . in a permissive society it is humbug to condemn prostitutes . . . people, happy in their personal pools, do not wish to be disturbed by outsiders who awake latent emotions . . . luck, at some stage, is a necessity for success . . . laws, aimed at improving human relations, will not force people to love each other . . . intellectuals are embarrassed by emotion . . . why should the majority wish to go beneath the surface of life? Gimmicks titillate and help them to get through the day, for this is the throw-away age, materially and spiritually . . . faith in economists and brilliant academics is like believing in Santa Claus . . . the magic of two people meeting for only a few minutes, but who seem to have known each other all their lives . . . the things you regret are those you have not had the courage to do . . . there can never be a just justice for all . . . too much knowledge takes away magic, and magic provides the excitement of life . . .

Then Oliver jumped off my lap and my reverie was over and I was back again into thinking about reality, about the broken panes of glass that I had replaced before breakfast by stapling the frames with polythene, and I wondered whether that frequent task was ever going to end. I watched Oliver go over to a patch of grass and start eating it, clumsily, like a cat who did not really like it. Then I stood up and moved away from my blue elvan rock and, instead of walking back up the track, I went on down towards the Folly Steps.

There are times in the far west of Cornwall when you can feel yourself enveloped by a mysticism which is not just a word, but an almost tangible communion with those who have been here before. Facts about Cornwall are interesting, fascinating, but there is another dimension that pervades and one does not have to be Cornish to be aware of it. The sensitive have the entry to this subtle cave, no age limits, no legal passport needed, just the awareness to feel, not to look, qualifies.

I walked away from my blue elvan rock and Oliver left his patch of grass; and I walked downwards to the meadow, the last of the Merlin cliff meadows, where a young man, who was once a tenant like myself of the land, saw a ghost . . . an old man in long-ago clothes and wearing a hat like a Quaker hat, who emerged out of the storm-pitted blue elvan rocks that shelter this meadow. No other person has seen this ghost, only the young man. But, not long after, he was staking bales of hay in his barn and a bale fell on him and he was killed.

I reached the bottom of the Folly Steps, so called because they took such hard work to dig that we nearly gave up half way, and I ejaculated: 'This is sheer folly!' . . . and so the word 'folly' went into our language. We are now delighted with our Folly Steps. They connect the Merlin cliff with the Minack cliff.

I clambered up them and, when I reached the top, I looked back for Oliver and found he had not followed me. I called and, after a minute or two, I saw him way down at the bottom. I called him again and he proceeded to scamper up the steps in the manner he had always done; then, when he had reached the top, he lay down. I went to him and picked him up.

'Oliver,' I said, 'nothing wrong with you, is there?'

He replied with a purr.

TWELVE

February . . . and my daily drive with the daffodils to Penzance Station had begun. We aimed to send our largest quantities for the end of the week market because, understandably, the market prices were then at their strongest. But, since we could not control nature, we had to keep pace with the daffodils by picking over the week-end and sending on Monday and Tuesday. The price for these sendings was invariably lower than at the end of the week, and this maddened us. We sent the daffodils in the pencil-bud stage . . . and so florists, having bought them at the lower price, could put them in cold store, then sell them at the higher weekend price in their shops.

On my journeys to and from Penzance Station, I would sometimes see my old friend Enoch Prowse, husband of Linda, and this year they had celebrated their golden wedding anniversary. One Friday I saw him loping down the hill after his daily visit to his son Owen's farm, part of which borders the lane on the way to Minack, and I drew up and called out to him: 'What a lovely day, Enoch!'

A cap was perched on his mop of white hair.

' "Lovely," you call it?'

'Yes, why not?'

'It won't be lovely for long . . . there's wind about.'

Then he paused.

'How are you doing?'

'Fine,' I said. 'Prices aren't all that good, but we're sending plenty away.'

'Don't work too hard, I tell you.'

'I won't, Enoch . . . but how's yourself?'

'My leg's not too good; some days better than others.'

Other people would see Enoch and stop and ask him for directions to this place or that, and sometimes they would ask him the way to Minack. He had a reply.

'Are your brakes safe?' he would say, directing them to our lane. 'They better be . . . or you'll end up in the briny!'

And there were those who would question him about the Merry Maidens, the circle of nineteen stones in a field on the left after passing the entrance to our lane. A stream of earnest people from all over the world come during the summer to stare at the Merry Maidens and to see the two giant granite pillars on the other side of the road. The Merry Maidens probably have a Druid origin, while the pillars are said by some to have been placed there by King Athelstan to celebrate the victory of his Saxon army over the Cornish at Boleigh, a battle that was fought around the site of Enoch's farm. Hence they are sometimes referred to as the Peace Stones.

But they are also called the Pipers, and this name is due to their legendary association with the Merry Maidens who, so generations of local children were warned, were nineteen young girls who defiled the Lord's Day by dancing to the music of the Pipers . . . and were transformed, along with the Pipers, into stone as a punishment.

A foreign visitor asked Enoch whether there was any truth in the legend.

Enoch, long accustomed to such questions, shrugged his shoulders and said: 'Can't tell you if it's true . . . but I've lived here over seventy years and I haven't seen any of they maidens dance yet.'

I arrived back that day for a late lunch and Jeannie had cheese sandwiches ready for me and a bottle of wine; and, because the day was so soft and warm, as if it were another day lent, we sat eating our sandwiches on the bridge.

'Enoch says there are winds about,' I said, 'and I saw Walter and he said the same.'

'They know,' said Jeannie. 'They're part of nature; they know the weather instinctively.'

Walter Grose is the one I call the pied-piper of cats. He shares the farm at the top of our lane with Jack and Alice Cockram. Jack and Alice have two clever daughters who, when they lived at the farm and were in the local school, used to bring the pile of birthday cards from the school on Fred's birthday. We have watched the two, Susan and Janet, grow up and fly away. Janet, after winning one scholarship after another from school to university, is now a dietician lecturer in London for a large firm. Jack, who helped to make this possible, is like all farmers in our area . . . working eighty and ninety hours a week.

Walter, much older than Jack, old enough long ago in Government theory to have retired, persists in working because he has worked all his life and finds a security in the routine. He lives, a bachelor, in the village of St Buryan, and comes daily to the farm in time for the early morning milking . . . and to be with his cats. The cats hide in the barns, in the outhouses, doze on stone walls but, when Walter in his yellow van appears, they too appear. And when he has his *croust*, or his midday meal, sitting in the van, you will find a gathering of cats around him, cats of all ages, of all colours, of every cat-coat design . . . and Walter is feeding them with Kitticat sandwiches.

'Do you feel happy?' I asked Jeannie.

We had been silent for a moment or two.

'Why do you suddenly ask that?'

'I know you . . . something's worrying you.'

'Any of us can be worrying all the time if we let our imaginations run free.'

'How is your particular imagination running free?'

Jeannie picked up the crumbs from her plate, pinching

164

the crumbs together with her fingers, so when she deposited them on the flat space of a nearby stone they resembled a pinch of salt.

'Oliver, I suppose . . . I don't know why, but I'm not happy about him.'

'His appetite is good enough.'

'That's true.'

My mind went back to the day when he and I went for a walk down the Merlin cliff; then I waited for him to scamper up the Folly Steps and he lay down when he reached the top. I remembered how, although it was not clear at the time to define, I had experienced a chill of concern.

'The only thing to do is to ask the vet to have a look at him and that will ease our minds,' I said.

'I'll call in on him on Monday morning,' Jeannie replied, picking up the bottle and filling my glass.

We can be watched by the donkeys, if they are in the big field above the cottage, as we sit on the bridge; and they were watching us on this occasion. Two heads close together above the little iron gate, ears pricked, staring, giving the impression that they were mentally trying to compel us to leave our chairs and walk over to them. No reaction from us and so, after a while, Fred began to bang his hoof against the gate, rattling it, and when this had no effect, he began to whinny and the whinny slowly changed into a hoot, which rose to a crescendo, shattering our peaceful lunch.

'What are you going to do?' asked Jeannie.

'Ignore them.'

'You can't . . . just look at them.'

Fred, head in the air, hoot at its highest note.

'Odd about Merlin,' I said. 'No hoot from him . . . nearly three years old and no hoot.'

'Perhaps he has nothing to hoot about.'

I laughed.

'Admit it. A silent donkey seems a bit strange.'

'Fred makes up for it.'

The shattering noise was over now and there they were, leaning over the gate, and I was enjoying my sandwiches and my glass of wine, but I had to suspend my enjoyment. I got up and went indoors and picked up a crust of brown bread that Jeannie had baked and came back and went up to the gate and gave it to them.

'You don't mind, do you?' I said to Jeannie, the donkeys already munching.

'Oh, no,' said Jeannie, charmingly, 'anything to keep the donkeys happy.'

They were happy in any case without Jeannie's bread. Fred and Merlin had become devoted friends and, when they grazed in the field, they were never far apart. At night, they lay on the grass side by side. What amused me was the way Fred had re-asserted his seniority, for when Merlin first arrived, the gusto of his youthful exuberance had driven Fred, for a while, into second place. No second place now. Bumptious Merlin had been quietened by Fred. Respect existed. When, for instance, after they had munched Jeannie's bread, I put on their halters with a view to leading them down to the stable meadow, it was Fred's halter I put on first and it was Fred who led the way. Worldly-wise Fred had educated Merlin. Discipline and respect were necessities for living, however tiresome they might appear to be. Fred, wild in his own youth, had tamed Merlin. Or had he? Merlin, I suspect, if he had a chance, would prove me wrong.

I came back after taking them down to the stable meadow, so sparing us from their gaze, and continued to enjoy my sandwiches. The bridge, with the space before it of the whole of Mount's Bay, of moorland on the other side of the valley, of the rim of the Lizard coastline, of silence except for the rumble of the sea and the birds with their occasional chatter, curlews soulfully calling their way towards Helford river, a raven grunting, a staccato call of a pheasant, always the gulls, always periodically Philip banging his beak on the porch glass . . . all these different sounds and sights come together into one's being and one cries out to oneself. Why, why, cannot the human race rid itself of envy and violence and petty momentary triumphs, and the vanity of its militant leaders, and rejoice in all the aspects of living that are free to be loved!

'Do you remember,' said Jeannie, 'Kim Foster standing here and looking across the valley and saying we must safeguard ourselves; be on watch that the land is not exploited?'

Kim Foster was for many years Chairman of the Cornwall County Council.

'I do.'

'Wouldn't it be terrible if some up-country developer got hold of it?'

'It would be the end of our lives here.'

'So many people have gone through the trauma of seeing their view of green fields turned into concrete.'

I drained my glass.

'Stop it, Jeannie,' I said. 'Your imagination is running too freely!'

She laughed.

'I'm not laughing at what you said, I'm laughing at the memory of our first sight of Oliver . . . up there in the corner of the field, when we watched him stalking and then he pounced and he missed!'

'I think we should always call it Oliver land over there.'

'I like that,' said Jeannie.

Friday afternoon during the daffodil season is time off for us, or rather it gives us a chance to catch up on some of the tasks that the rush of the week has stopped us from doing. That particular Friday, however, the afternoon was so gentle and pleasant that we resisted doing the tasks we ought to have done and went a walk after our sandwich lunch to Carn Barges, the cascade of rocks that we see falling to the sea as we sit on the bridge. We had reached it, the sea below us smooth as a table, the sun in our eyes as we looked back at the cottage, the air still, when suddenly the sky was filled with a concourse of gulls, rising higher and higher, calling anguished cries, circling above us, hundred upon hundreds, until I said to Jeannie that they resembled a mammoth gathering of starlings. Then, on this gentle day which seemed like a day lent, there was a sudden breeze.

'Did you hear the forecast?' I said.

'No, I didn't.'

'The weather is changing.'

'Judging by the gulls, you're right.'

Gulls sense storms. Gulls, when they begin to soar into the sky, calling out their weird cries which old people used to say were the cries of lost sailors, are giving a warning. They are flying away from the rocks where massive waves will smash and flying inland to fields where they will cluster, heads towards the winds, defiant.

We returned to the cottage and I went about my pre-evening tasks of collecting logs and the phurnacite, the potatoes for supper, and picking the brussels sprouts, and gathering an armful of hay and carrying it to the shelter of the stables, where Merlin tried to seize it before I entered. Inside the cottage, Jeannie had roast beef on the evening menu.

'Jeannie,' I said, 'roast beef, just what I long for tonight!'

As I spoke, there was a slap of a noise from our bedroom.

'That's the window,' Jeannie said.

'The wind opening the window.'

'Come up suddenly.'

'It always does.'

'I would like a bath,' said Jeannie, 'and I've used

all the hot water for washing up so I can't have one.'

Hot water comes from our open-fire boiler, but we also have Calor gas in the bathroom to heat an Ascot water heater. But when the wind blows strongly from the west, it blows out the jets of the Ascot water heater.

'Where's Ambrose?'

'You know where Oliver is; he's on the Heatstore, but Ambrose . . .'

I had a hunch he might have followed me and I went back to the porch door and, when I opened it, Ambrose rushed in and so fast that it would seem he had been leaning against the door. I shut the door quickly. I was glad he was with us. It was comforting that everyone at Minack had been accounted for as the winds began to blow.

I relished Jeannie's roast beef and the blackberry tart and her own Cornish cream that accompanied it . . . and all the time outside the rushing noise was increasing.

'Did you hear that?' I said suddenly.

'It came from the chimney.'

'It was a sort of guttural sound.'

When the winds blow there is a cacophony of sounds which are probably explainable, but which set the imagination alight.

'Don't want the chimney to fall on us!' said Jeannie.

'It's the greenhouses I'm terrified of!'

'Nothing we can do . . . nothing.'

Oliver continued to sleep on the storage heater. Ambrose prowled, then went to the door, miaowing.

'You're *not* going out, Ambrose.'

We went to bed early and, because I was scared of the roar outside, I put plugs in my ears and slept so well that it was daylight when I woke.

It was much colder. The gale had swung away from the west, was coming from the east, from the Lizard, attacking the front of the cottage, attacking the greenhouses where their defences were weakest, where there was no wood to shelter them.

'How did you sleep, Jeannie?'

'Hardly at all . . . I thought the roof was coming off!'

'You've got Oliver beside you.'

'He purred during the night so loudly that he almost drowned the noise of the wind! Ambrose was here, too, until a few minutes ago.'

I put out my hand and touched Oliver and he gave me one of his peculiar little yaps of appreciation.

'I'm glad we're asking the vet to come out and see him on Monday.'

'We're wise to get him, I'm certain. It may be nothing, but . . .'

We were both silent for a few moments.

'Are you going to get up then?' asked Jeannie.

'I don't dare!'

'You'll have to see what's happened to the greenhouses sooner or later.'

'This is the beginning. It's been blowing for only twelve hours and a storm like this always goes on for forty-eight hours . . . another thirty-six hours to go!'

'Just look from the window.'

I still did not move. Anything to delay what I might find.

'All right,' I said, at last. 'I'll make the effort.'

I got up, put on my dressing gown and walked over to the window by my writing desk from where I had a view of the Orlyt.

'At least three large panes in the roof have gone,' I called back to Jeannie.

I was quite calm. I was indeed surprised how calm I felt. It was the soothing sensation that can come to people who are involved in a calamity, a calamity in progress.

'I'm going to dress,' I added, 'and go down to see the donkeys and then I'll have a walk round.'

'Take special care.'

'I will.'

There was nothing I could do. I found Fred and Merlin in the stables and I was reassured to find them apparently content. They still had some of the hay lying in a corner which I had brought to them when the storm began. But there was nothing I could do about the damage I found had already been done to the Orlyt and one of the greenhouses which Joe Coward, the Midlands business man who became a labourer, warned me, when I was planning to erect them, would become a millstone around my neck. That greenhouse appeared from a distance, from the nearest spot I dared go to look at it for fear of flying glass, to be shattered.

Yet it was the Orlyt which presented the most fearsome sight. It was so fearsome that my calmness, the calmness of people involved in a calamity, was threatened. Not three panes in the roof had gone, but four or five . . . and a whole stretch of the side of the Orlyt which bordered the lane, the side which faced the full ferocity of the storm as it roared across the sea from the Lizard, had come apart from its base and was swaying, both frame and glass, in the wind.

Torrential rain was now falling when I returned to Jeannie.

'All I can say, Jeannie,' I commented, as I sat down on the sofa, 'is that I now have an inkling what long-distance sailors go through in small yachts.'

Thirty-six hours of the storm to go at my guess. I intended to keep away from the greenhouses. Broken glass can fly in a storm like dislodged slates. I was remembering the storm when Jane, of *A Drake at the Door*, came over from Tresco Gardens in the Scillies and won the Prince of Wales's Cup for the finest box of daffodils at the Penzance Flower Show. She was the youngest competitor ever to do so . . . and the storm, the raging storm, coming as this one from the east, nearly stopped her from taking to the Show the Carbineer daffodils which she had put overnight, because she was staying with us for the event, in the Orlyt. The storm that afternoon was swaying the whole Orlyt and I had told her and Jeannie, as I left them to go into Penzance, that they should not risk opening the Orlyt door. As soon as I was out of sight, they did open it, thank goodness . . . and the Carbineers won Jane, sixteen years old, the Prince of Wales's Cup.

There was nothing we could do except wait.

Nothing we could do except become accustomed to the noise, the threats, the strange sense of acceptance that nature was dictating our lives, not man, not a computer, not academics, not intellectuals. These, with all their brains, were impotent.

BBC radio announced trees down over main roads and power lines down and areas blacked out. At three forty-five on Saturday afternoon, as I was trying to escape from the roar outside by watching a race meeting on television, the programme was interrupted by a warning that weather equivalent to a cyclone was expected in Devon and Cornwall, resulting in structural damage. No sign of snow here . . . but in Devon, Somerset and Dorset there was the worst blizzard in thirty years, with Taunton, Exeter and Lynmouth cut off.

Wait, wait, wait . . .

We sat cocooned in the cottage, reading, pretending life was normal.

'Oliver's off his food,' said Jeannie.

'The storm has put him off it.'

Jeannie was over by the storage heater, tempting Oliver with freshly-cooked coley.

'Come on, Oliver. This is good for you.'

But Oliver turned his head away.

Wait, wait, wait . . .

We went to bed early, ear plugs again hiding me from my fears. Then up on Sunday morning prepared to find the Orlyt a crushed mass of broken glass. We went to look together.

'It's still there!'

The side, forty feet of it, was still swaying in the wind, much of the glass smashed, but miraculously the roof was still holding.

'Jeannie,' I said, holding her hand, 'it's going to survive!'

All through the morning, all through the afternoon and into the evening, the winds continued to blow . . . until at nightfall, as if a tap had been turned off, there was a sudden stillness.

Our world seemed at peace again.

The Orlyt was patched up, polythene sheets draped over it, pending full repair; and on the green bolster, their favourite place in the greenhouse, Ambrose huddled close to Oliver as he had done so many, many times before. They were warm there in the sun.

The vet had come on the Monday after the storm was over, and he had come several times since. We were expecting him again any minute. Oliver was suffering no pain, his life was just ebbing away; and in our hearts we knew that this would be the vet's last visit.

As I waited, I remembered that first time I saw Oliver, in the corner of the field on the other side of the valley which we now call Oliver land; and I remembered too, that Sunday morning when I stood by Monty's Leap, and out of the undergrowth appeared the tiny ginger kitten.

I wondered, as I looked at the two of them, how Ambrose would manage on his own.